MW00637070

FROST
A HUSKER'S JOURNEY HOME

WRITERS

DIRK CHATELAIN
Sports Writer

CHRIS HEADY
Sports Writer

LEE BARFKNECHT
Sports Writer

EVAN BLAND
Sports Writer

SAM McKEWON
Sports Writer

TOM SHATEL
Sports Columnist

EDITORS
Kristine Gerber and Thad Livingston

DESIGNER
Christine Zueck-Watkins

COPY EDITORS
Stu Pospisil and Doug Thomas

PHOTOGRAPHERS
Listed on page 160

STORIES FROM OUR ARCHIVES
Jack Bailey, James Denney, Rich Kaipust, Colleen Kenney, Paul Hammel, Gregg McBride, Elizabeth Merrill, Eric Olson, Stu Pospisil, Wally Provost and Conde Sargent

PHOTOGRAPHY ASSISTANCE
Jeff Bundy
Barrett Stinson, Grand Island Independent
Matt Haley, Atlanta Falcons
Larry and Carol Frost
University of Northern Iowa

RESEARCH ASSISTANCE
Ben Egger, Wood River High School
Matt Gideon, Wood River, Nebraska
Steve Glenn, The Shelton Clipper

PRINT AND PRODUCTION COORDINATORS
Pat "Murphy" Benoit and Bryan Kroenke

MARKETING AND FULFILLMENT
Michelle Gullett and Rich Warren

A PRODUCT OF THE OMAHA WORLD-HERALD
President Phil Taylor
Vice President for News Mike Reilly
Executive Editor Melissa Matczak

Omaha World-Herald, 1314 Douglas St., Omaha, NE 68102-1811   omaha.com l owhstore.com

First Edition ISBN: 978-1-7322317-1-9   Printed by Walsworth Publishing Co.

ON THE COVER:
April 21, 2018: Scott Frost at the Nebraska spring game at Memorial Stadium.

ON THE BACK COVER:
Jan. 29, 1993: Scott in Wood River on the day he announces he is committing to Stanford.

ON THE TITLE PAGE:
April 21, 2018: Scott leads the Huskers during the Tunnel Walk prior to the Nebraska spring game at Memorial Stadium.

AT RIGHT:
Sept. 7, 1996: Scott's first start at Nebraska, where the Huskers beat Michigan State 55-14 in Lincoln.

FIRST STEPS

BY DIRK CHATELAIN

THE FOURTH-GRADERS ARE IN HEAVEN. It's field trip day at Memorial Stadium, a muggy Tuesday in May. They follow the red carpet from the Nebraska locker room to the northwest corner of the field. Then they take off, dashing to the south end zone like Nebraska wide receiver Stanley Morgan.

The 50 ... the 40 ... the 30 ... the 20 ... the 10 ... TOUCHDOWN!

They spin and shout, eventually jogging back to midfield, where they surround the big red "N" and listen to their official tour guide present a history lesson of this hallowed ground. One class leaves and another comes. Repeat scene. There's something about the turf under their shoes that gives 10-year-olds a sugar high.

Not one of them looks up to the bleachers and notices the sweaty, shirtless man in a Chicago Cubs hat. The man who quarterbacked Nebraska to its last national championship before they were born. The man charged with reviving Husker football for the next generation.

Scott Frost.

*April 21, 2018: Nebraska coach
Scott Frost waves to fans following the
spring game at Memorial Stadium.*

The head coach began his exercise at 11:44 a.m. He strapped a 40-pound black weight vest over his shoulders and followed a 26-year-old assistant — offensive analyst Dustin Haines — up the concrete steps between sections 32 and 33 in North Stadium. All the way to the top.

They turn right, catch their breath and head for the aisle separating section 33 and 34. They descend from the 99th row and turn for the next section. Over. Up. Over. Down.

One week later, Frost will hike the Grand Canyon in front of ESPN cameras, 24 miles rim to rim, dropping and then rising nearly 5,000 feet. Consider today a practice workout.

Over. Up. Over. Down. It's a little bit different from Tom Osborne's exercise routine, isn't it. The legend who won 255 games in 25 seasons spent countless hours — brutally hot ones in July and bitterly cold ones in December — jogging around this field that now bears his name. Thinking about how to beat Colorado and Oklahoma and Miami.

On Jan. 2, 1998, the same night that Frost last wore his red No. 7, Osborne walked away for good. Nebraskans expected the machine to keep rolling. It did not. Over the past 16 seasons — 2002-17 — four head coaches have been fired and 79 games have been lost. The program has accumulated too many humiliations to count.

As Nebraska football slipped further and further from national relevance, the sense of desperation intensified. Who could possibly restore it? What characteristics were necessary? What does it take?

By Thanksgiving 2017, all eyes focused on Frost. In theory, thousands of Nebraska football players could've been qualified to lift the Big Red out of this grand canyon. But the man who shunned Osborne as an 18-year-old recruit was the resounding choice.

Why?

This book tells the extraordinary story of a native son who, whether he knew it or not, was destined to be Osborne's heir, even before he was born. Frost was blessed with unique athletic genes and environments that nurtured his gifts. But he also endured struggle, pain and betrayal. Together, his experiences gave him a foundation that even Osborne didn't have as a new head coach in 1973.

You'll find it in remarkable detail. A narrative of the Frost family dating back to the 1940s. A scrapbook of archival stories and photos even the most ardent fans haven't seen. An examination of Frost's most pivotal years and how they led him back home.

The book details his mother's heroic path to the 1968 Olympics and his father's influence on the Bob Devaney era. It sheds light on Scott's high school exploits, including a playoff game that still amazes Wood River teammates. It details his falling

out at Stanford, his scout-team fights with the Peter brothers and how Frost won over the fan base again, then won the national championship.

If it all had ended 20 years ago in Miami, Frost's life would've been worthy of reflection. But he wasn't on the short list of Nebraska's most popular alums — not even close. What happened afterward is the real reason he's here now. NFL coaches Todd Bowles, Mike Tomlin and Bill Belichick share accounts of Frost's appetite to learn. Former Oregon coach Mike Bellotti recounts the 25-minute meeting that changed Frost's career trajectory.

As Nebraska drifted from the blueprint that made it great, Frost was quietly bridging the gap between him and his dream job.

Rubbing shoulders with coaches Bill Parcells, Monte Kiffin and Chip Kelly stopped being a fun bit of trivia for friends back home and started looking like a master's course in coaching. The vision came into focus in 2017 when Central Florida, two years removed from a winless season, won nine more football games than Nebraska did. Nine!

It's too soon to call Frost the savior in Lincoln — or even a success — but his first 43 years look like the perfect training ground for the hike in front of him.

Just after noon inside Memorial Stadium, Frost passes his grandparents' old seats, the ones they bought two years after World War II. Section 7, row 2, seats 14 and 15.

He's halfway done with his workout and feeling the pain. The sun is poking through the clouds. Sweat soaks through his hat. He grabs railings to pull himself up.

When he finishes the East Stadium, he follows his guide to the South for the longest climbs. The aisles are 98 rows high and when Frost reaches section 16A, he stops several times and plants his hands on his knees.

Behind him, the elementary kids are dancing on the turf. Posing for pictures. Making snow angels in the north end zone — one rolls to his stomach and executes the worm dance. Frost keeps going.

By the time he reaches the West Stadium, his old wideout and wingman, Matt Davison, is on the turf heckling him. They're supposed to play golf when Frost is finished.

"Let's go!" says Davison, sweat-free and smiling. "Time to tee off."

Over. Up. Over. Down. The last grade-schoolers clear the field. The cathedral is silent.

At 12:40 p.m., after 1.83 miles, 56 minutes and about 5,000 steps, Frost opens a gate and steps onto the turf, just a few paces from the northwest tunnel he'll enter on fall Saturdays. He unstraps the weight vest and immediately becomes 40 pounds lighter.

"You ready to go?" Davison asks. Frost buries his hands into his knees, panting. The journey is complete. Another one is just beginning. Frost cracks a smile.

"Might need some water."

The two-story crow's nest is one of the last remnants of
Malcolm High School's former football field where a chance
meeting in 1964 between athletes Larry Frost and Carol
Moseke still carries weight more than half a century later.

THE MEETING IN MALCOLM

————————

LARRY AND CAROL FROST

BY DIRK CHATELAIN

THIRTEEN MILES NORTHWEST of Memorial Stadium, the past disappears in a jungle of steel and weeds.

Step out of the car and into the spring sunshine. Feel a gentle breeze blowing out of the south. Hear the robins singing in the trees.

Was it really here on the east edge of Malcolm? Yes, it must have been. Most everything from 50 years ago is gone: the scoreboard at the north end, the dirt track encircling the field, the pickups that parked within feet of the chain gang, waiting to honk their horns when the star running back scored another touchdown — he scored 41 his senior year.

Look closely, though, and you can still see little bits of evidence. Like the broken long jump runway down the home team sideline. Follow that path past the rusted machinery that pokes up from the weeds like steel skeletons.

Past a combine cab with broken windows and occupied by flies. Past old tractor tires and rolled-up chain-link fence, a 300-gallon fuel tank and strips of telephone poles, hose and pipe, stones and trusses collecting last night's rain. A red grain wagon labeled with white spray paint — "Gene."

Gene is nowhere to be found. Nor is anyone else. Somehow in 20 years since it ceased to host Friday night gatherings, the old Malcolm High School football field became a depository for junk.

Only imagination brings it all back to life.

Up the hill to the east, the two-story public announcer's booth — the crow's nest — still stands, but the windows are gone. One lies in the tall grass 15 feet below.

Before it, there's a stand of bleachers — eight rows, 30 yards long — with young pine trees growing up between the boards. Duck under the steel railing — the white paint is long chipped away — and step toward the top. Careful now, the boards are rotten, like trap doors. One misstep leads to a crash.

Climb to the top. Feel the breeze again. Picture a spring afternoon in 1964 and a meeting that still carries weight more than half a century later.

CAROL JEAN MOSEKE was a freshman at the University of Nebraska-Lincoln. A standout in track and field who'd already competed all over the country, including the Los Angeles Coliseum, where she received a medal from a brash Olympic boxing champion. But UNL didn't allow her to practice on its track, so her coach had to escort her to local high schools.

Before Nebraska officially sanctioned girls track and field, Carol competed on the AAU circuit with the Cedar Rapids Road Runners.

On this day, they came to Malcolm, arriving after the high school track and field team finished training. There was just one kid left on the field, the hardest-working boy at Malcolm.

Larry Frost wandered over to a couple of college girls throwing the shot put and made small talk. Who's your big star, he asked. They pointed at the blond throwing the javelin.

Larry approached Carol. Let's see who can throw this spear farther. They spent the next few minutes heaving it back and forth.

"He was absolutely sure that he could throw the javelin farther than I could," Carol said.

Isn't this how all romances start?

That spring, America was whipping itself into a frenzy. The Beatles exploded on the radio. Ford Motor Co. released the Mustang. Women read "The Feminine Mystique." Vietnam heated up and the Senate debated the Civil Rights Act. LBJ preached the war on poverty and Malcolm X preached black nationalism. Americans, still grieving over Dallas, wondered who really killed JFK.

Institutions came under assault. Hierarchies began to crumble. Young clashed with old.

Carol and Larry were mostly insulated from all of that. They were cut from the same cultural cloth: shy, humble, self-motivated farm kids who grew up working the fields and chasing balls. They flourished in small towns and became two of the best high school athletes in the state.

But they were different, too. Very different.

Larry Frost's childhood dreams were already mapped out. In 1964, Bob Devaney's resurgent program cast a long shadow in Nebraska and Larry wanted to follow the native sons to Memorial Stadium.

Carol Moseke didn't have sports heroes, at least not of her gender. She was mocked in Cedar Rapids, Nebraska for being a tomboy, evicted from her UNL dormitory, relegated to the pig barns at the Nebraska State Fairgrounds to train. She was a pioneer.

Following their meeting in Malcolm, Larry and Carol stayed in touch. Their first date was a University High basketball game. They hunted and fished and watched movies. When Carol umpired softball games in Lincoln, Larry showed up to tease her – *"That was a strike!"* Afterward, they grabbed chili dogs at King's Drive-In.

Four years later, during his junior season at Nebraska and one month before she marched in the Olympic opening ceremonies in Mexico City, Larry drove Carol back to Malcolm and dropped to a knee on the shot put ring.

Romance? That's more like it.

SEPTEMBER 26, 1968

ROMANCE BLOOMS FOR ATHLETIC PAIR

BY WALLY PROVOST

Some of my best friends don't believe me but I know a halfback who is planning to marry a discus thrower.

After dating for more than a year, the couple became engaged several weeks ago.

Athletic ability adds to the compatibility. For example, the couple worked out together during a family vacation in Minnesota the past summer. The halfback served as retriever for the discus thrower. The latter passed the football while the halfback brushed up on his receiving.

The halfback returns to Minnesota this week with the University of Nebraska football team. He is Larry Frost, who leads the Huskers in pass catches.

Larry's fiancé, Lincoln school teacher Carol Moseke, will compete Sunday in an Olympic Games tune-up track meet at Flagstaff, Ariz.

Miss Moseke qualified for the Mexico City Olympics by throwing the discus 178 feet one week after receiving her engagement ring. Her part-time tutor, Randall Lambert of Ainsworth, says that is the best distance by an American woman this year.

Chances for an Olympic medal are not lustrous, however. East and West Germany each has a gal who has bettered 200 feet. A couple of Russians have been in the 190s.

Miss Moseke has been weightlifting and running cross country on alternate mornings at the U.S. women's team camp at Los Alamos N.M. Afternoons, she sails the discus and does some sprinting.

Halfback Frost's future bride assuredly will represent this country to the best of her ability.

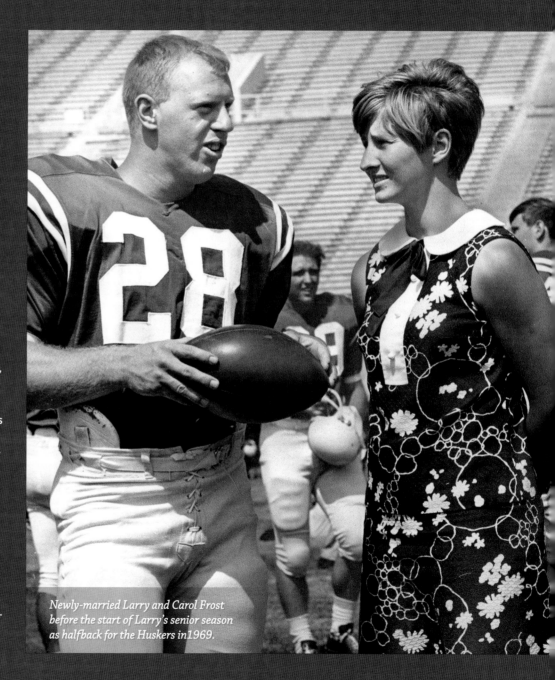

Newly-married Larry and Carol Frost before the start of Larry's senior season as halfback for the Huskers in 1969.

THE IMAGE STICKS WITH HER almost 60 years later. Her hometown school. The little gymnasium. A few rows near the court, then a balcony above.

On winter nights after school, Carol Moseke walked in, sat where no one noticed her and watched the boys basketball team practice. One thought flashed in her head over and over, like a light that nobody else saw.

March 20, 1964

Carol, above, outscores the entire opposing team in an AAU game in 1964. She is a member of the AAU Women's Basketball Hall of Fame.

I could do that.

Teenage girls in the 1960s weren't getting opportunities to do that, not in basketball or much of anything else. Didn't matter if you were potentially the best athlete in the state.

But one thing, looking back, is indisputable. Carol would've had no chance in Omaha or Lincoln or Grand Island, which were even less progressive toward girls sports. She made a name for herself because she grew up in a town of 512 people. A town like Cedar Rapids.

Joe and Marie Moseke (pronounced MOSE-a-key) bounced around in the '40s and '50s, renting farmland from big landowners. Occasionally they moved without a choice because the owner sold the land under their feet.

Her father, Joe, eventually found 600 acres on a big hill five miles southeast of Cedar Rapids. Half was pastureland, half was farmland. The Mosekes split the profits with the owner.

They had two girls, a boy, then a 6-year gap before Carol Jean came along.

Her older sisters grew up helping mom in the house. Not Carol.

The farmhouse was 200 yards from the cattle barn. Twice a day, Carol milked cows by hand, then toted the 5-gallon buckets to the house, where she descended to the cold, dirt-floor basement and separated cream from milk. On Saturday nights, they loaded into the family car, took the cream to town and made a few bucks.

When Carol wasn't working, she shadowed her brother. To the corn crib, where they played basketball in the winter.

"I had a sweet jumper," Carol said.

To the backyard, where 16-year-old Jerry coaxed 10-year-old Carol to catch his fastballs. Picture little sis squatting like Yogi Berra. The difference? Her old mitt didn't have padding, so she wore a work glove underneath to soften the blow.

Jerry was no slouch. He'd later walk on to Jerry Bush's Nebraska basketball team. But Carol was the real talent. If she matched her brother's chores on the farm, why couldn't she play sports like him, too?

According to Jerry, she could've been the starting point guard for the boys basketball team — the girls didn't have a team. And the starting shortstop for the boys Junior American Legion team.

How many times did she throw her rubber softball off the foundation of the farmhouse, scoop it up and whip it back against the wall like she was throwing to first base?

"Millions," she said.

Carol had one more gift she never got a chance to show a crowd: She could throw a football. One day in the schoolyard, Carol and Patti Gulley were playing touch football when it got a little too physical.

"I remember getting in her way once," Gulley said. "You stopped making that mistake."

LARRY FROST'S LITTLE COUSIN followed him everywhere on the Woodlawn farm. To the yard, where they played baseball and softball. To the second floor of the barn, where Larry had built a basketball court.

The only place Doug Parrott had a chance to beat Larry was in the living room playing electric football. Or so he thought.

You remember the game? Line up your plastic little football figures on a metal gridiron. Flip the switch and let the vibration move the players across the board, hopefully in the right direction.

Larry, maybe 10 years old, was drubbing his 6-year-old cousin one day when Doug's dad intervened. Dangit, can you let him win just once?

On the next play, Larry lined up all his blockers on one side of the board, leaving just a runner behind the center. They flipped the switch, the board started buzzing and the sea of defenders parted.

"Somehow he got through all of my guys and scored a touchdown," Parrott said.

That was Larry. So good he didn't have to try. Of course, he always tried.

Larry's ancestors first settled the area in 1869, two years after Nebraska achieved statehood. By the 1920s, his maternal grandfather, a carpenter and future mayor, built the family house on Exeter Street in Malcolm, where bats swooped down from the catalpa trees.

Larry's mom, Opal, grew up watching farmers herd cattle into the town stockyards. She gathered with friends on summer Saturday nights to watch movies on the projector screen that hung from the shady side of the community hall. She caught magic shows at Joe Woodard's garage and avoided the traveling gypsies. Opal was a standout athlete herself: a force on the volleyball court and the Lincoln city tennis champion.

In the depths of the Great Depression, she kept newspaper clippings of Nebraska football. The Huskers won eight Big Six titles from 1928-37.

Lawrence, was three years younger than Opal. His unusual hair inspired the childhood nickname "white top." Eventually it got shortened to "Top" and stuck. His parents managed the dairy in Woodlawn, a little outpost along Highway 34, north-west of where the Lincoln Airport is now. The farm was owned by Lincoln's William H. Ferguson, who has been described as the Warren Buffett of his day. Ferguson is the namesake of a mansion near the State Capitol.

Scott's grandfather, "Top" Frost.

Top was more a man of the people. He may have been a standout athlete, too, but he graduated from Lincoln High at 14 years old. He served in World War II and fought in Europe, leading a mortar squad — Scott Frost wore grandpa's dog tags at his wedding in 2016.

When he came home, he was a socialite known for his bib overalls. He frequented the Malcolm pool hall. He hosted wiener roasts at the farm. He volunteered on the fire department. He was a natural seed corn salesman. Oh, and he filled his bowling team with the best talent he could find.

"He generally had all the good ones," former neighbor Larry England said.

In 1947, Top and Opal's only child arrived with an unfortunate surprise. A cleft palate that eventually caused a speech impediment.

Larry's football success at Malcolm High School attracts the attention of college recruiters, including Nebraska receivers coach Tom Osborne, who came to Malcolm in 1964 to watch him play. "He carried the ball six times and he scored six touchdowns," Osborne would remember.

Larry kept to himself as a kid, but his legs never stopped moving. The farm was home base — his dad managed the dairy during Larry's early years — and the youngest Frost was active in everything from 4-H to the Lincoln Police Department's midget football league. He learned to read and write at Woodlawn's one-room schoolhouse, the same one his father attended, walking the railroad to classes each morning.

He nearly chose Lincoln High, but his roots were in Malcolm. In high school, he was "one of those natural leaders," Stan Schulz said. Active in National Honor Society, Student Council, one-act plays, vocal music and speech — he received a superior rating for "Discussion" his junior year.

For all his success — let's not forget homecoming king — Larry kept a level head and a clear priority.

"It was sports, sports, sports," said Russ Schmersal, Malcolm class of '66.

Larry scored 41 points in a basketball game against Bennet — Malcolm put up 108. He broke track and field school records in the 100-yard dash (10.0), 220 (22.5), broad jump (20-11½), triple jump (37-3½), shot put (47-1) and discus (147-0).

"I'd always see him do the quarter mile, the 220 and the 100," Schmersal said. "Then we go to a track meet and he's throwing the discus and shot put. I couldn't figure out what he's doing. I'd never seen him do that before. Oh, he said, when I get done, I go home and practice."

Then there was football, where he was often the fastest and strongest player on the field.

"When he was carrying the ball, it was like a freight train," Schmersal said. "I tackled him one time in practice. Jeepers, I was looking out the ear hole of my helmet. My chin was scuffed up."

"It was almost painful to watch how much bigger, stronger, faster he was than those kids in eight-man football," said Parrott, Larry's cousin.

In the fall of '64, word of Larry's exploits got back to Lincoln. That's when Tom Osborne showed up.

IN HIGH SCHOOL, LARRY BROKE TRACK AND FIELD SCHOOL RECORDS IN THE 100-YARD DASH, 220, BROAD JUMP, TRIPLE JUMP, SHOT PUT AND DISCUS.

FEBRUARY 21, 1965

DEVANEY: NEED MORE LIKE HIM

BY WALLY PROVOST

You may not believe this story...

So as a starter, let's just pretend there is a 17-year-old high school senior who is active in speech, debate, chorus, drama. He fits into this column because he also is a four-sport athlete.

He plays football — 121 touchdowns' worth in four seasons. This makes him fit into the dream world of a number of college coaches.

The young man has an IQ of 125, which he has exercised in becoming a high-ranking scholar.

He scores touchdowns and he doesn't have to be wet nursed in the classroom. Hot item? You bet. Colorado's Eddie Crowder was among the coaches who thought so.

Crowder visited the athlete at his high school and at his farm home about six miles northwest of Lincoln. Said the coach: "We'd like you to visit us in Boulder. Look over the campus, the athletic facilities. At our expense, of course."

The athlete politely declined. Later he explained:

"I didn't think it was fair to let them spend the money on me. I knew where I was going to university — Nebraska. I figured some other kid might as well have the trip."

DEVANEY TESTIFIES

Coach Eldon Lindquist at Malcom High School insists such a boy does exist. He says his name is Larry Frost.

Coach Bob Devaney at Nebraska backs up Coach Lindquist, noting that Larry was the first football player to sign a letter of intent with the Huskers this year.

"We wish more boys in Nebraska felt the way Larry does about his state university," Coach Devaney remarked. His loyalties are with Nebraska. This is the school he wants to represent.

"And in the long run, of course, this is the place where the most interest will be show in him — during school and in the years that follow."

Larry Frost is a six-footer weighing 195 pounds. "He is a hard runner," said Coach Lindquist. "He doubled as linebacker and probably was the best defensive player I had."

Larry netted 1,917 yards rushing his senior season. He scored 41 touchdowns; totaled 255 points.

In track, he runs the 100 and 440, puts the shot and does some broad jumping. Last year he placed second in the state Class D 100 with a time of 10.1. He took second in the shot at the Lancaster County Track Meet.

He currently is averaging about 20 points in basketball. Friday night he broke the school record with an output of 41 points at Bennet.

Last summer, he quit fooling around. He attended Boys State, played centerfield in Legion baseball, raised and showed 4-H calves, managed a kid baseball team and coached a girls softball team.

TOUGH ENOUGH

Can Larry make the transition from eight-man football to the more complicated 11-man game? "There won't be anybody working harder, and I think he's tough enough to play in the Big Eight," said Coach Lindquist.

"He's a big strong kid with good speed and good desire," said Coach Devaney. "From all we've found out, he learns quickly."

Devaney added that an eight-man graduate fared well at Wyoming U. while he was coach there. "His name is Jerry Hill. He's now the No. 1 fullback with the Baltimore Colts."

Says Larry: "I played four years of 11-man football with the team sponsored by the Police Department in Lincoln's midget league. I really don't see a lot of difference. I hope I can make it."

One more question Larry. When did you first have the idea that you wanted to play football at Nebraska?

"Since I was about four..."

If there really is a Larry Frost, I think he'll make the grade.

Larry, with former Nebraska assistant coach Clete Fischer, signs his letter of intent to play football for the Cornhuskers.

The high school state track meet at Memorial Stadium where Larry medals in the 100- and 220-yard dashes. He likes to remind Scott that he holds the Frost family record in the 100, with a time of 10.0.

The Cedar Rapids High School Road Runners team in 1962. From left: Patti Webster, Bonnie Yilk, Carol Moseke and Sue Van De Walle.

SHE WOULD'VE BEEN a small-town folk hero, but nothing more. The girl a generation ahead of her time who inspired stories in the Cedar Valley Conference.

You think such-and-such girl is good? You should've seen Carol Moseke.

That was her fate until spring of 11th grade, when her world opened.

The Cedar Rapids girls played softball in the summer and fall — Carol led the team to a state championship. In the winter, they played volleyball before the boys basketball games — Carol hustled into the locker room and swapped her jersey for a cheerleading skirt.

Come spring, there was nothing for girls to do. That's when Randall Lambert got an idea: girls track.

The English teacher and boys basketball coach, inspired by Carol's talent, hauled four girls to the Batenhorst gravel pit. He marked off specific distances on the road between the lake and the Cedar River. Lambert grabbed his stopwatch and put the girls through a workout they'd never experienced. Wind sprints.

"When we played softball and volleyball, nobody made us run wind sprints," said Patti Gulley, a team member. "He just kept running us till we thought we were gonna drop."

Lambert called them the Road Runners and they returned every day because the school wouldn't allow them to practice with the boys track team — Nebraska hadn't yet sanctioned girls track.

They bought white button-up blouses, went to the home economics room and found the biggest canning pot. They heated water, inserted dye and — voila! — their white blouses matched Cedar Rapids' school color: gold.

"Those were our first uniforms," Gulley said.

They ironed "Road Runners" on the back of sweatshirts, found some maroon shorts and headed for one of Nebraska's first AAU girls track meets, in Cozad. As far west as Carol had ever been.

At another meet in Fremont, Carol scored 50.5 of the team's 89 points, winning the shot put, discus and 880-yard run. She got second in the low hurdles, second in baseball throw, tied for fourth in high jump and ran anchor on the third-place 440-relay team.

Carol and Patti did well enough that first spring to qualify for the National AAU Girls and Women's Track and Field Championships in Los Angeles. Everyone, including Carol's mom and dad, was skeptical when Lambert packed the station wagon.

Her parents didn't miss her softball and volleyball games, but track and field seemed silly. Carol went anyway.

En route to California, they scaled the Rocky Mountains and sweated through the Mojave Desert — remember, no air conditioning — and stopped at the Grand Canyon. Picture this 17-year-old farm girl walking up to the world's greatest chasm.

"It was kinda like Chevy Chase," Gulley said. "They walk up to the edge, he kinda bobs his head a few times and says, 'OK, let's go.' That was kinda what we did."

In California, they visited the ocean and stayed at a University of Southern California dormitory, rooming next to a few Japanese girls.

Carol, still unsure of her gifts, did OK in the hurdles and 880. But she had few peers in throwing events. She finished second in the shot put — 38 feet, 11½ inches — and heaved the discus far enough to win (130-11), if only it had landed in bounds.

When she returned to Nebraska, she quit hurdles and races and committed to throwing. She taught herself with technical diagrams in library books. She watched teaching films. She recorded herself on a little Super 8 film camera.

The 100,000-seat Los Angeles Coliseum had opened her eyes to the world. She wanted more. Before leaving the American landmark on July 8, 1962, Carol received her shiny silver medal in the shot put, placed around her neck by an Olympic champion, a man who, over the next 15 years, would go down as the most famous athlete in the world. Some might even say the greatest.

Cassius Clay.

THE RED-HEADED RECEIVERS COACH got the recruiting assignment in the fall of 1964, just as Nebraska football was surging to a 9-0 start.

There's a kid in Malcolm I want you to go watch, Bob Devaney told him. So Tom Osborne, 27 years old, rolled up Highway 34 on a Friday night in search of a record-breaking, eight-man standout.

Larry Frost didn't need a sales pitch. His dad, Top, was a true believer in Nebraska football. He'd purchased season tickets in 1947 when he returned from the war and stood by the Huskers during the lowly '50s. Larry wanted to be a Husker even before he attended his first day at Woodlawn schoolhouse.

By '64, he was making a mockery of Class D. His statistics were almost comical: 1,917 rushing yards on just 144 carries, an average of 13.3 per rush. He busted off runs of 78, 76 and 75 yards, pretty good for an 80-yard field. Twice he scored seven touchdowns in a game. He finished the season with 41.

When Osborne arrived at the Malcolm field that night in 1964, he hadn't seen many eight-man football games. Nor many Larry Frosts.

"He carried the ball six times and he scored six touchdowns," Osborne said.

Osborne didn't need to twist Bob Devaney's arm to offer the kid a scholarship. And Frost didn't waste any time saying yes. He was so committed that he didn't bother taking free recruiting visits to other Big Eight schools.

Frost's publicity grew the next spring during track season. On April 12, 1965, he appeared in The World-Herald in Gregg McBride's column, next to a report from The Masters, where Jack Nicklaus had just shattered the scoring record at 17-under.

"Larry Frost of Malcolm is the best big boy rolling over the Nebraska high school cinders this spring," McBride wrote.

In the span of an hour at the Midland Relays, Frost covered 100 yards in 10.2 seconds, ran the 440 in 52.1, broad jumped 20-11½, heaved the shot put 45-9½ and the discus 137-11.

Somehow he won none of those events at the state meet at Memorial Stadium, getting clipped in the 100 for the third straight year.

"Oh, he was madder than a hornet," Parrott said.

(Larry forgave himself; for years he teased his son, Scott, that he owned a faster 100 time.)

Frost was still a small-town mystery until Aug. 22, 1965. That's when he broke free for a 74-yard touchdown run at the Shrine Bowl, the only score of the game.

August 22, 1965

Frost Scamper Chills North All-Stars, 7-0

Eight-Man Grad Sparkles as South Surprises in Shrine Grid Classic

By Gregg McBride
World-Herald Sports Staff Member

Memorial Stadium, Lincoln — No Nebraska high school football player ever made a more spectacular debut in eleven-man ball than Larry Frost of little Malcolm High School Saturday.

Frost, tagged by The World-Herald last November as one of the state's all-time eight-man greats, ran 74 yards for the third-quarter touchdown which gave the South a 7-to-0 victory and a 5-to-2 bulge in the Shrine Bowl series.

The crowd of 18 thousand found the 70-degree temperature under overcast sky pleasing for August.

However, R. C. (Bob) Russell, president of the Shrine Bowl, estimated a threat of rain cut the crowd by five or six thousand and the profit to Shrines hospitals for crippled children to slightly over 60 thousand dollars.

Frost, getting the big boost from his touchdown sprint, plunged and ran 115 yards.

This was almost half his team's rushing total, more than twice the yardage of his teammate Bob Scott and almost triple the gain charted by Dick Davis, Omaha North Athlete of the Year Award winner.

WEARING NO. 30, LARRY PLAYS HIS FIRST 11-MAN FOOTBALL GAME AT THE 1965 SHRINE BOWL WHERE HIS 74-YARD TOUCHDOWN, RIGHT, WON THE GAME. HE RECEIVES THE MOST VALUABLE PLAYER AWARD, THE FIRST CLASS D PLAYER TO EARN THE HONOR. IN 1983, THE 25TH SHRINE BOWL ANNIVERSARY COMMITTEE HONORS LARRY BY NAMING HIM ONE OF 25 PLAYERS TO THE ALL-STAR TEAM.

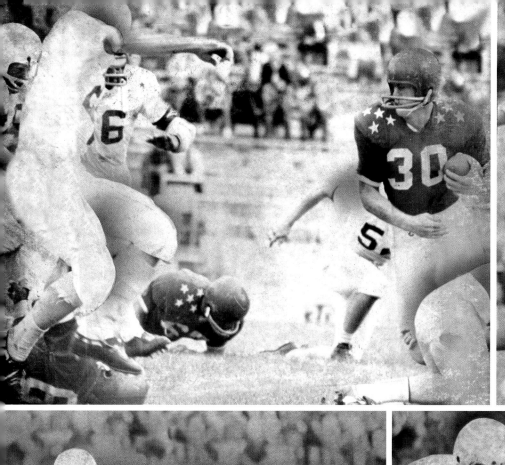

THEY HEARD THE CATCALLS and rumors. They noticed the looks of mockery and envy. The Cedar Rapids Road Runners, like Nebraska pioneers a century earlier, learned quickly that progress didn't come without resistance.

Teenage girls in 1962 were training to be teachers, hairdressers, secretaries and housewives, not Olympians. They weren't supposed to be sweating at the gravel pit every afternoon.

Had the girls never amounted to anything, nobody in Cedar Rapids would've cared. They might have laughed, Bonnie Burghardt said. But now the Road Runners were appearing on a local TV station. They were showing up in the Omaha World-Herald.

"The problem was, because of Carol Jean, we started getting our names in the paper," said Burghardt, Carol's cousin and Road Runners teammate.

The Road Runners were competing at the region's best track meets and coming home with medals. People back home preferred Friday night football.

"We got the pat on the head and the boys got the steak dinner," Burghardt said.

Carol kept her mouth shut and her eyes forward. Her family didn't have money to send her to college, but she took Advanced Placement correspondence courses and scored a Regents Scholarship to Nebraska.

She caught another break when Mr. Lambert landed the superintendent job at Garland — just 25 miles from Lincoln. He kept coaching the Road Runners, picking up a Roberts Dairy sponsorship and adding to the roster with the best talent in Nebraska.

One day, they stopped in Omaha to pick up a Central High sprinter named Deborah Alston, and her little sister. Didn't matter that they were black and the Road Runners were white.

"Now I think, oh my word, that must have taken so much courage for them and also for her parents," Gulley said. "But we hit it off."

Lambert drove the brown and tan station wagon — eight or nine girls crammed in back — as far as Kalispell, Montana, for the AAU junior nationals. Carol's local legend grew as she climbed the national charts.

By '65, she made her first national team. She traveled to Poland, Germany and Russia, competing in a Kiev stadium packed with fans and flowers.

"But on the far side was this mammoth poster of Lenin," Carol said.

Carol's biggest resistance came not in Red Square, where the American team was followed. It came back home in the shadow of Memorial Stadium, where university leaders had no interest in women's sports.

The head of the physical education department was an old lady with gray hair in a bun.

"She was absolutely sure that women should not compete," Carol said.

She wasn't alone. Female students had to wear skirts or dresses to class. They couldn't appear on campus with rollers in their hair. Freshmen at Pound Hall had a 9 p.m. curfew.

Carol had no interest in leading a feminist revolt. She hated when girls played the victim, she just wanted to compete. The athletic department wouldn't let her train on the track, so she drove to Lincoln high schools.

Sometimes she walked up 14th Street to the Nebraska Fairgrounds and practiced alone in the pig barn, stashing her shot, discus and javelin where no one could find them. She didn't have a toe board or a painted circle. She threw off a concrete slab where tractors parked.

When it was too cold to walk, she ran the 13 flights of Pound Hall.

COACH RANDALL LAMBERT

BY DIRK CHATELAIN

Randall Lambert was only 26 years old, but he knew a phenom when he saw one. So the Cedar Rapids English teacher packed up his station wagon, headed for the gravel pit and started a track team — a girls track and field team.

No one made a greater imprint on Carol Moseke's career than Lambert.

He grew up in Winfield, Kansas, and graduated from the University of Nebraska-Lincoln, where he was sports editor of The Daily Nebraskan. His initial coaching interest was boys basketball — he coached the Cedar Rapids boys. But Moseke's "one in a million" talent inspired Lambert.

He spent the next decade absorbed in girls track and field as he climbed the ladder in educational administration. Lambert was instrumental in pushing Nebraska high schools to sanction the girls.

"We still have a few school administrators who think it isn't ladylike to have sports for girls," he said in 1971. "I disagree with them."

That spring, May 15, 1971, the Nebraska Schools Activities Association held the first girls state track meet in Grand Island. Almost 300 schools participated, including the Gothenburg team that Carol started. It's worth noting that only 18 Class A schools were there — the city schools were more restrictive of girls.

North Platte won Class A. Blair captured Class B. Hastings St. Cecilia won Class C. Thedford took Class D.

"The success of the meet probably will result in state meet competition soon in other sports, particularly volleyball and perhaps tennis and golf," The World-Herald's Conde Sargent wrote.

Lambert's influence catapulted Moseke to the '68 Olympics. Four years later, Lambert made it, too, serving as an assistant on the '72 Olympic team. His role? Women's field events coach.

When Lambert started in the spring of '62, he knew nothing about throwing a discus or a shot put. By '72, he was America's expert.

Lambert eventually took an administration job out of state and died a decade later in a Colorado car accident. Carol Frost remembers him with reverence.

She still calls him "Mr. Lambert."

CAROL ATTENDS THE UNIVERSITY OF NEBRASKA ON A REGENTS SCHOLARSHIP. HER HIGH SCHOOL TRACK AND FIELD COACH, RANDALL LAMBERT, PICTURED ABOVE, ENCOURAGES HER TO ATTEND. SHE CONTINUES TO COMPETE UNDER LAMBERT THROUGHOUT COLLEGE, AND HIS INFLUENCE HELPS PROPEL CAROL ONTO NATIONAL- AND INTERNATIONAL-LEVEL COMPETITION.

AAU STAR IS BOTH STRONG AND FEMININE

BY JACK BAILEY

CEDAR RAPIDS — Two of Nebraska's proudest parents are Mr. and Mrs. Joe Moseke. Their daughter, Carol, is one the hottest "weight girls" to come along in the Women's National AAU in many years.

Just a couple of weeks ago, she placed first in the discus in the Women's National AAU, second in the javelin and sixth in the shot put.

... The buttons just about pop off the shirt of her dad when her name is mentioned. Her mother is a wee bit more reserved but she doesn't want anyone to get the impression that because Carol handles the weight events and plays softball with the agility of many boys, she has lost her femininity.

"Carol can be very feminine when she wants to and she can be awfully boyish," Mrs Moseke said. "She isn't a very big girl but she is well proportioned. When she dresses up she's very much a lady."

..."She can do anything on the farm and do most of it better than the average person," her dad says proudly. "I wouldn't be afraid to start her out in the spring putting in the crops and let her take care of them right though the harvest. I know she'd come up with a bumper crop.

"Carol's been riding a tractor ever since she was in grade school. She can handle anything you put behind it. A few years ago we had a lot of dairy cattle and Carol did all the milking."

... Mrs. Moseke spoke up then and said the youthful track star is pretty handy in the kitchen also. She said Carol is an excellent cook and a good housekeeper. Carol's only weak point around the house, her mother confessed, is her sewing. She doesn't care too much about that.

Whenever Carol comes home, even if it's only for a day, if there is work to be done in the field she will be found in the field doing it, Mr. Moseke said. He said this happened last week when he was cutting hay. Carol came home, donned her work clothes and was in the hay field on a tractor in front of a rake.

AMATEUR ATHLETIC UNION
OF THE UNITED STATES

Certificate of Selection

1966 ALL-AMERICA WOMEN'S TRACK AND FIELD TEAM
Selected by the Women's National Track and Field Committee

WOMEN'S DIVISION

Event	Name	Club
80 Meter Hurdles	CHERRIE SHERRARD	Laurel Track Club
200 Meter Hurdles	PAT VAN WOLVELAERE	Angles Track Club
100 Yard Dash	WYOMIA TYUS	Tennessee State
200 Yard Dash	EDITH McGUIRE	Tennessee State
440 Yard Run	CHARLETTE COOKE	Los Angeles Mercurettes
880 Yard Run	CHARLETTE COOKE	Los Angeles Mercurettes
1500 Meter Run	DORIS BROWN	Falcon Track Club
Long Jump	WILLYE WHITE	Mayor Daley Youth Foundation
High Jump	ELEANOR MONTGOMERY	Tennessee State
4 Kilo Shot Put	LYNN GRAHAM	Southern Pacific AAU
Discus	CAROL MOSEKE	Midwestern AAU
Javelin	ReNAE BAIR	San Diego Track Club
Pentathlon	PAT WINSLOW	San Mateo Track Club

GIRL'S DIVISION

Event	Name	Club
50 Yard Hurdle	DENISE PASCHAL	Laurel Track Club
50 Yard Dash	PERNETTA GLENN	Compton Track Club
100 Yard Dash	PERNETTA GLENN	Compton Track Club
220 Yard Dash	GEORGIA JOHNSON	Metro Track Club
440 Yard Run	KATHY HAMMOND	Will's Spikettes
880 Yard Run	DINO LOWREY	Will's Spikettes
Long Jump	BETHE McBRIDE	Liberty Athletic Club
High Jump	DIANE WATERS	Frederick, Maryland
8-lb. Shot Put	MAREN SEIDLER	Georgia AAU
Discus	RANEE KETCHKA	Midwestern AAU
Javelin	BARBARA FRIEDRICH	Shore Athletic Club

New York, January 1, 1967

Clifford H. Buck, *PRESIDENT*   Stephen M. Carlin, *SECRETARY*   *CHAIRMAN, WOMEN'S TRACK AND FIELD COMMITTEE*

In 1966, Carol represents the United States in AAU international competition. Her throw of 161 feet, 3 inches in the discus is the best in the country and earns her All-America AAU honors.

After two years working various jobs — washing dishes in the dorm kitchen and operating the telephone switchboard — Carol had worked her way to Pound Hall residence director. Then the woman in charge kicked her out. Why?

She didn't like to see Carol sweating after workouts.

Image was always part of the story. Even her supporters couldn't resist describing her looks. From Gregg McBride's June 1966 Omaha World-Herald column:

"Miss Moseke, in addition to boasting athletic ability, has the face and form to make her a popular ambassador of women's track in Nebraska. Her 148 pounds are well distributed over a durable frame, and her pretty face always carries a contagious smile."

In '66, she was the national discus champion. In '67, she won gold at the Pan-Am Games in Canada. Then in '68, one week after Larry proposed, she became the first Nebraska woman to qualify for the Olympics, reaching the standard with a mark of 178 feet. Her personal best.

For all her success, Carol's parents never experienced a big meet. Money was tight and her mother had diabetes. Her biggest fan was Larry, who had built her two discus rings — one in Cedar Rapids, one in Woodlawn.

On Oct. 18, 1968, Larry summoned the nerve to ask Bob Devaney if he could skip the team's pre-game movie in downtown Lincoln — the Huskers hosted Missouri the following day — so he could watch Carol throw the discus in Mexico City.

She never appeared on TV, failing to advance past the preliminary round. The Russians and East Germans were doping without consequence in those days. As they lifted weights in Olympic factories, Carol was hoisting a bar and a few dumbbells back in Nebraska.

But she represented her country. She marched into the stadium in her white dress with black and red chevrons. She watched Bob Beamon long jump 29 feet. She saw Dick Fosbury's innovative flop. She saw John Carlos and Tommie Smith raise their fists in protest. She, too, performed in front

of the world's best athletes, reaching a level that still seems preposterous 50 years later.

In 1962, Carol Moseke was running wind sprints on a sandy road next to a gravel pit outside Cedar Rapids. Six years later, with little help back home, she was one of 83 American women to call herself an Olympian.

The Grand Canyon didn't seem so big anymore.

Carol wins gold in the discus at the 1967 Pan-Am Games.

CAROL MOSEKE — BRAWN AND BEAUTY

BY JAMES DENNEY

Back in the good old days when grandma was a kid, Nebraska girls were permitted to play high school basketball, run on the track and even participate in softball.

Then the local busybodies took a look and viewed with alarm the sight of grandma running around in her bloomers.

So organized athletics, on the female front, came to an end. But, as with milady's hemline, time brings changes in sport, too, and along with progress has come a more liberal policy in permitting young ladies to complete.

Though today's physical education experts haven't said so, part of the change is due to the poor showing of the United States feminine representatives in the World Olympics.

Until recently, our fairer sex has been clobbered by the likes of the Soviet Union and other Iron Curtain countries.

HERE IN NEBRASKA, the change in outlook toward feminine competitors in high school (Iowa has had girls' basketball for years) has been gradual. It started with volleyball and has spread to track and field.

C.C. Thompson, executive secretary of the Nebraska School Activities Association, disclosed that regulations of his organization do not prohibit girls' track or volleyball.

"The association prohibits only boxing and basketball for girls," said Thompson. "In fact, and I hope it never comes to this, schools in Nebraska could have girls' football teams if they desired."

The association, governing body of all inter-school activities in the state, does not permit girls to compete on boys' teams. "This rule would prohibit a girl place kicker from playing football. It also denies girl golfers or tennis play-ers from being on boys' teams," said Thompson.

The Amateur Athletic Union and John F. Kennedy College of Wahoo "have provided some of the current drive for more girls' sports in Nebraska," added Thompson. JFK completed in the National AAU Girls Basketball Tournament this year.

ONE YOUNG LADY who certainly has enjoyed the fruits of the new popularity in girls' sports is Miss Carol Jean Moseke, 22-year-old University of Nebraska senior from Cedar Rapids, Neb.

... Does girls' track have a future in this state for misses like Carol Jean?

"I think it does," said Al Riddington, sports editor of the Beatrice Sun and one of the chief promoters of the annual AAU meet held in his community.

C. C. Thompson certainly doesn't believe the High School Activities Association will be a roadblock.

"We do not have to approve dual or triangular meets," he said. "We do approve the invitational and I have noticed that there have been more this year than ever before."

THERE IS NO "girls' state sports championship," sponsored by the NHSAA, as such. Peru State College annually holds a volleyball "state championship."

"The question of whether girls district and state track meets will become necessary," said Thompson, "will depend upon the schools themselves, There seems to be more interest but the school would have to decide and petition for district and state meets."

For Carol Jean Moseke, it's all been a "wonderful experience, thanks to Mr. Lambert (her coach). I think there is a place for girls' track and I think if we have more competitors, we can catch the Russians."

Program from the 1968 Olympics in Mexico City, where Carol competes in the discus.

IN 1968, CAROL, WITH A PERSONAL-BEST THROW OF 178 FEET IN THE DISCUS, BECOMES THE FIRST NEBRASKA WOMAN TO QUALIFY FOR THE OLYMPICS. SHE FINISHES 14TH COMPETING AGAINST THE RUSSIANS, EAST GERMANS AND ROMANIANS, WHO WERE HAND SELECTED WHEN THEY WERE YOUNG AND TRAINED EXTENSIVELY.

Carol Moseke on the cover of the Omaha World-Herald's Magazine of the Midlands in 1967.

Larry in 1969, his senior year. It was said Larry could block like a tight end, catch like a receiver and run like an I-back. Offensive coordinator Tom Osborne uses all of those skills.

NEBRASKA DIDN'T HAVE video boards, but it had a Tunnel Walk.

Once Bob Devaney finished his pre-game pep talk, the Huskers filed out of Schulte Fieldhouse — they would've run through the brick wall had coach asked them. They tapped their lucky horseshoe, reached the north end zone and absorbed the Memorial Stadium cheers. Behold another sellout crowd of 65,000-plus.

It was more than Larry Frost's stomach could handle. He made a beeline to the sideline and vomited in the trash can. It happened more than once.

"Sometimes it took him a little while," teammate Bill Bomberger said. "So we'd form a line around him so that the people in the stands didn't have to see it. We gave out a big cheer when Larry finally tossed his cookies. We knew we were ready to go."

Frost had his skeptics when he came to Lincoln in 1965. The jump from eight-man football to the Big Eight was broader than he imagined. For four years, Larry struggled, bouncing from halfback to flanker to linebacker to tight end. Nothing fit quite right.

He didn't complain, sticking to his quiet ways. "Larry was about the nicest guy we ever had," Bomberger said. But it looked like he might end his career without making an impact.

Then came 1969. Frost was married, mature and motivated. He spent the summer catching balls from Carol. Thanks to Osborne, he finally had a position.

The Huskers had gone 6-4 in '67 and again in '68. The latter season ended with a 47-0 blowout loss at Oklahoma on national television, the worst defeat of Devaney's career.

Back home that winter, Osborne said, "there was a fair amount of heat."

Devaney didn't just hope for a rebound. He made it happen, asking his play-caller to modernize the stagnant Husker offense. Osborne did his research and shelved the unbalanced line and full-house backfield in exchange for an I-formation attack with spread concepts.

Sept. 20, 1969 Nebraska vs. USC at Memorial Stadium: Larry's 36-yard gain set up a Husker touchdown three plays later.

Oct. 25, 1969 Nebraska vs. Oklahoma State at Memorial Stadium:
Larry, No. 28, has a clear path through the Cowboy defense to the end zone.

The addition of Jerry Tagge, Van Brownson, Jeff Kinney and Bob Newton helped. So did the incorporation of a senior wingback whom Osborne had recruited five years earlier in Malcolm. Frost could block like a tight end, catch like a receiver and run like an I-back. Osborne utilized all of those skills.

The offense took off. Following a 2-2 start, Nebraska won seven straight, including a 44-14 drubbing of Oklahoma in Norman.

"I don't think I ever saw Bob (Devaney) happier," receiver Guy Ingles said, "even after the Orange Bowl win the next year."

Ingles and others credit the '69 seniors for paving the way for the '70 national championship season. Truth is, the Huskers were playing as well as anyone in the country by the end of '69.

They finished their careers in El Paso, Texas — not quite as exotic as Miami — where they crushed the Georgia Bulldogs in the Sun Bowl, 45-6.

Larry receives the outstanding senior offensive back award from the Optimist Clubs of Lincoln.

Frost, from the Rodeway Inn where the Huskers stayed that week, reflected on a career that didn't start as he planned.

"When I enrolled at Nebraska, I probably thought — like most guys, I suppose — that I was going to set the world on fire.

"And there were times when I wished I had gone to a smaller school where I would have had the opportunity to play more.

"I would have to say without question or doubt that this year has made up for it all. Playing first string for a Big Eight championship team at Nebraska is all I ever could have dreamed. I wouldn't trade it for four years of All-America at a smaller school."

THE NEXT FALL, 1970, Larry watched the Huskers — with some help from his wingback replacement, Johnny Rodgers — win the program's first national championship.

It was Year One of a 44-year coaching career that would take him to almost every kind of school in Nebraska — and a few outside the state.

Carol made sacrifices for that life.

In the summer of 1970, she threw the discus 169-2 in Cozad, 15 feet better than the American leader. Surely she could've made a second Olympics in '72. But starting a family was more important, and Steve was born a few months before the Munich Games.

From 1976-80, Carol was the Nebraska women's track and field coach. When she arrived, her salary was $2,000 and the program was losing prospects to Kearney State College. Three years later, she beat out Texas Woman's University for future Jamaican Olympian Merlene Ottey. A watershed moment for the program.

She gave it up to follow Larry's career.

"I made a choice for the family and for the kids and their school," she said. "It was just too much. You're gone all the time."

Larry entered a tough situation at O'Neill in 1980. His only assistant was a line coach. He needed help, especially if he wanted to open up the offense and throw the ball as he wished. Whom did he call on?

"I had been throwing to him ever since he was at the university," Carol said. "Outs, horns, hooks and everything. He recruited me to coach the receivers."

GOTHENBURG BUYS A FROSTY PACKAGE

BY CONDE SARGENT

What high school pep club in Nebraska this fall will be directed by any individual with Olympic Games experience? **Answer:** Gothenburg.

Larry, Gothenburg's new coach, in 1970.

Question: Why is that?

Answer: Because Larry Frost was hired this week by the Board of Education.

Q: Is Frost going to direct the pep club.

A: No, you dummy you, he's going to coach the football team. His wife, Carol, America's 1968 women's Olympic discus thrower, also has been hired by the school system. She'll run the pep club and teach girls' physical education.

Q: Is that what you'll call a package deal?

A: It certainly is, according to the enthusiastic words from Gothenburg. If hard work wins football games, Gothenburg's going to have it made.

Carol in 1971. At Gothenburg, she teaches physical education and starts the girls track and field team.

Bob Devaney had Tom Osborne. Larry Frost had Carol Frost.

For the next 30 years, she coached his receivers and defensive ends. She received plenty of strange looks when she showed up on a new sideline, especially in Texas.

That is where the Frosts introduced their second son to youth sports. Scott was in second grade when he played his first football game. Wingback, just like his dad. The first time he touched the ball, he went 70 yards for a touchdown.

"He just had speed," Carol said.

Their situation in Palestine was prosperous and they might have stayed forever. But Top Frost died in 1985 and Larry, an only child, didn't want to be so far away from his mother. They moved back to Nebraska, packing the baby book that Carol made for Scott.

It includes all the little landmarks a mother keeps. But there's something unusual inside. Something that "shows you how nuts we are," Carol said.

The Bob Devaney Sports Center was brand new when Carol accepted the Nebraska track and field job. Her youngest son was 18 months old. Imagine him trying to lift his first shot put as Carol mentored Merlene Ottey.

One day Scott and Steve were playing in the long jump pit at the Devaney Center when Frank Sevigne's 400-meter runners dashed around the final curve at top speed. Little Scott wandered onto the track and nearly got run over by a pack of Jamaicans.

Sevigne was irate at Carol. "I deserved to get yelled at. But I couldn't afford a babysitter."

Scott was 2 when Carol got an idea. She mapped out a 40-yard dash on the track and grabbed a stopwatch, beginning a routine that continued until he graduated high school. Every year, she marked the results in his baby book, charting the progression.

Nine seconds ... eight seconds ... seven ... six ... five ...

Yes, nature provided Scott Frost a head start on his competition. But don't forget: He was nurtured to be great, too.

WHERE COACHING TOOK THE FROSTS

1970-71
Gothenburg

1972-74
Crete

1975
Park Hill, Kansas City

1976-79
Lincoln High

1980-81
O'Neill

1982-85
Palestine, Texas

1986-88
McCook

1989-98
Wood River

1999-2000
Shenandoah, Iowa

2001-2005
Walthill

2006-07; 2011-13
Lincoln Parkview Christian

Carol and Larry in 2002 at Walthill, Nebraska.

COACHING WAS A TEAM EFFORT FOR CAROL AND LARRY. IN THE FALL, LARRY WAS HEAD FOOTBALL COACH AND CAROL WAS THE ASSISTANT COACH IN CHARGE OF RECEIVERS AND DEFENSIVE ENDS. THE ROLE REVERSED IN THE SPRING WITH CAROL THE HEAD TRACK COACH AND LARRY HER ASSISTANT.

AN EARLY ATHLETE

Scott was born Jan. 4, 1975 in Lincoln, the second son of Larry and Carol. According to his parents, he showed athleticism from an early age.

"The thing about Scott, believe this or not — and most people don't — is he has never had an ounce of fat on his body," Larry told Omaha World-Herald reporter Colleen Kenney in 1997. "As a baby, a newborn, he had muscle definement. He was hard as a rock." When Scott was about 7 months old, his parents had to pack their baby's crib away. "Steve would stay in the crib," Larry said. "Ninety-nine percent of the babies in the world stay in the crib. But Scott, he'd just drop to the floor and crawl wherever he wanted to go."

According to Larry, Scott's favorite quarterback when he was young was Bob Griese, an All-American at Purdue who later lead the Miami Dolphins to Super Bowl victories in 1973 and 1974. Scott called him "Bob Geesey."

In elementary school, Scott played basketball, No. 1 above, and football, right, in Palestine, Texas.

"Scott had developed a lazy eye when he was about a year old, and he had to wear real thick, heavy glasses for a couple of years to straighten that out," Larry said. The only way we could get him to wear his glasses was to remind him that 'Bob Geesey' wore glasses."

Scott was a second-grader in Texas when he started playing youth football. First time he touched the ball, he ran about 70 yards. "Scott has his head on right," Larry said in 1996. "He has played football since he was in the second grade. He knows the important thing is to give your best effort."

ACCORDING TO LARRY IN A 1997 ARTICLE, SCOTT AND STEVE GREW UP BILINGUAL: ENGLISH AND SPORTS. AT THE DINNER TABLE, THE FOUR FROSTS TALKED STRATEGY AND PLAYS.

Scott played football as a seventh- and eighth-grader in McCook, Nebraska. Scott competed twice in the pentathlon at the National Junior Olympics. In July 1987, in Provo, Utah, he placed first in the 80-meter hurdles, second in the shot put, fifth in the high jump, second in the long jump and sixth in the 1,500-meter run. He earned a second-place medal in the 11-12 year-old division with 2,396 points. He was coached by his mom, Carol.

The Wood River High School football field and track in 2018. From 1989 through 1993, Scott Frost competes here in both sports.

WONDERS IN WOOD RIVER

_____

HIGH SCHOOL: 1989-93

BY CHRIS HEADY

THE SOUND OF CLEATS clicked and echoed off the walls inside Wood River High School as Scott Frost and the Eagles made their walk from the locker room to the brown steel door.

That November night was chilly, somewhere in the 20s, with light fog lingering overhead. The door swung open and Frost was hit with a rush of cold air and met by squealing fans bundled and shivering under the bleachers. The sight of Frost and the 7-2 Eagles whipped locals into a frenzy. They slapped helmets and shoulder pads as the Eagles weaved through the crowd to the field for warm-ups.

The Wood River fight song rang out into the night as Matt Gideon, a junior wide receiver, turned back to look at the crowd. The 11 rows of bleachers were packed. Encircling the field, four rows of fans leaned against the chain-link fence, stretching the entirety of the 400-meter track. Trucks were parked on the grass near the shot put circle. Gideon looked

east, above remnants of weathered cornstalks, and saw parked cars on the side of the road stretching a mile into the distance. Fans marched down Wood River Road, cutting through the evening fog toward the stadium for the Class C-1 playoff game between Wood River and Hastings St. Cecilia.

There must have been 5,000 people there that night, Gideon guessed. And it might as well have been a dream. This was not the Wood River he knew.

The Wood River he grew up in was not a destination for casual football fans around the state, let alone big-time college football coaches. It was a tiny 1,100-person, no-stoplight town along U.S. Highway 30 nestled between the bigger cities of Grand Island and Kearney and surrounded by omnipresent fields of corn.

But from 1989 to 1993, Wood River was a destination.

During those years, Frost and his parents built a small-town football dynasty. ESPN visited. The town showed up in newspapers across the country, even in Sports Illustrated. It became the place to be for college coaches like Lou Holtz and Bill Walsh who were looking for a quarterback.

If you look closely, more than 20 years later, there is still proof of that transformation.

A bumper sticker with Scott's name was recently slapped on the Wood River sign entering town. At the high school, there are new bleachers painted shiny silver, but an older, rustier set remains with beams of fading purple from the time when the town would quadruple in size just so fans could catch a glimpse of No. 7.

The same purple scoreboard stands at attention near the end zone. The press box is still teal. The hurdles for track practice have the 1992 Olympics emblem on them, brought by Scott's mom, Carol Frost, when she was the track coach.

Inside the school, a small photo of Scott is glued to the Class of 1993 composite. He smiles in a navy sport coat and red tie, surrounded by his 47 classmates. There's a shrine near the cafeteria, his purple jersey carefully folded in a frame. His school records, untouched, likely to remain that way, well, forever, hang near the cafeteria. Behind the athletic director's desk, there are plaques from those days: Male Athlete of the Year by The World-Herald, Gatorade Player of the Year, 1992 All-American selection by Schutt Sports, 1992-1993 All-America High School Football Team by Parade Magazine.

Around town, he's still known as the blonde boy wonder. The stories of his Bunyanesque feats are passed down, farmer to farmer, seniors to freshmen. When he comes to town now, it's news, and it spreads quickly. When he's talked about, there's a sense of familiarity and ownership.

He's known not as the Nebraska head coach. Not as the former national champion quarterback or NFL safety.

He's known, simply, as Scott.

Scott excels in football, track and field and basketball at Wood River High School. The hallways display his plaques and football jersey. His records still stand.

AT THE BANG of the starter's pistol, 12-year-old Scott took off down the track.

Bursting with power over the first hurdle and gliding over the next seven with Olympic technique taught by his mother, he crossed the line in an age-group record time, qualifying him for the 1987 State Junior Olympics finals in Columbus.

Scott, the athlete, had arrived in Nebraska.

"He's been hearing it from his father and me since he first dribbled a YMCA basketball or played little league football, about how to handle pressure, how to lead, how to outwork your opponent," Carol said in 1987. "For us, those have been daily conversations."

A few weeks later, Scott placed second nationally — for the second time in three years — in the Junior Olympics pentathlon, falling just short of a gold medal.

Scott wasn't satisfied.

None of the Frosts will lose, Carol said, "without a major fight."

Which was more true for Scott than anyone. One time, when the Frosts were in Texas playing a family game of Monopoly, Scott landed on Park Place and had to pay up. He smacked the table so hard, he gashed his hand.

The Frosts landed back in the Nebraska in 1986, when Larry accepted a job at McCook High School. They moved from Palestine, Texas, where Larry and Carol coached for four seasons. The McCook job was Larry's fifth stop as a coach in Nebraska, and it only lasted three years. In 1989, he accepted the job at Wood River.

It was a position, by most accounts, that would require some serious rebuilding.

"As a school, the culture of Wood River football, it was kinda low at that point," said Gideon.

The last real success the school had in football was in 1984, when the Eagles made it to the state playoffs, but lost in the first round. Wood River entered the 1985 season ranked No. 10 in the state, but started the season 1-4.

From 1986 to 1988, Wood River only won three games, finishing 3-23 over three seasons. In 1987, the school moved from Class B to C-1 and still went 0-9. From 1987 to 1988, the Eagles lost 16 straight games.

Then, in 1989, Larry and Carol took over. Almost immediately, things changed.

Larry implemented a weight training program, the first of its kind in Wood River. He and Carol installed a veer offense, similar to what Nebraska ran under Tom Osborne. They showed film of old NFL games at their house and invited players to watch.

And with them, Larry and Carol brought their sons: Steve and Scott.

Steve was a junior and played on the offensive line. Some center, some tackle.

Scott was a freshman, but was head and shoulders larger than every other 14-year-old rookie.

"As far as his physical stature, and speed and everything, he was just better than everyone. Way better," Gideon said.

Steve Spiehs, a classmate of Scott's, remembers when the Frosts moved to town in 1989 before Scott's freshman year. Some older Wood River players, Spiehs said, weren't huge fans of Scott. They saw the young quarterback as someone who needed to be knocked down a few pegs.

That didn't happen.

Within months, Spiehs said, Scott won over most of the team. In part because Scott was just so much better than everyone else and showed he was willing to outwork anyone on the team.

The veer offense came naturally to Scott, who at that age was running around a 5.0 40-yard dash and had been taught to throw by his Olympian mother.

But even so, as a freshman in 1989, Scott had to wait his turn. Senior Brian Packer got the nod from Larry to be the Game One starter against Centura.

That didn't go well.

After a quarter and a half, Packer couldn't get the Wood River offense going. Down 14-0, Larry called his son off the bench.

Scott hit wide receiver Derek Aptel for his first touchdown to make it 14-7. Then, in the third, Scott found Shane Pitts on fourth and long to make it 14-14.

But the Eagles lost, 28-14.

In Game Two, Packer got the start again. But in a sloppy, rainy, muddy game against Hastings St. Cecilia, Scott took over.

In the fourth quarter, he rumbled in from three yards for his second rushing touchdown to put Wood River up 14-7. He sealed the win with an interception, giving the Eagles their first victory of the season.

And from that moment forward, the starting spot was Scott's.

Wood River finished the year 4-5. Scott threw for 837 yards and 11 touchdowns. On the ground, he added 275 yards and 18 touchdowns.

Good numbers for a freshman.

Curiosity around Nebraska was piqued.

TOM OSBORNE'S COMMENTS ON SCOTT'S PERFORMANCE AT THE 1990 NEBRASKA FOOTBALL SCHOOL.

> COACHES COMMENTS:
> You have excellent athletic gifts for a sophomore. I hope that you will continue to work on your throwing regularly — also keep active in the weight room and in working on your speed.
> Good luck, Tom Osborne

Football Family: It was all football for the Frost family in August 1992. Scott starts his senior season as Wood River's quarterback; older brother, Steve, plays on the offensive line at Colorado State; dad, Larry, is head football coach at Wood River; and mom, Carol, coaches the receivers.

Aug. 31, 1990: Scott, No. 7, guides the Eagles to 513 yards of total offense in a 40-15 victory over Centura. The 6-foot-2, 180-pound sophomore completes 15 of 23 passes for 180 yards and four touchdowns and runs for 106 yards.

Wood River's 1990 season began again against Centura, where Scott threw for 180 yards and four touchdowns and ran for 106 yards in the 40-15 win.

The sophomore became a problem for teams around the state. It took just five games for him to eclipse 1,000 yards rushing, and the quarterback was starting to develop a killer instinct.

On Oct. 14, 1990, against Ravenna, Wood River led 20-0 right before halftime.

With six seconds left at his own 30-yard line, instead of handing the ball off and running out the clock, Scott audibled to a quarterback draw.

"I thought he may be a little crazy when I heard the call," Larry would say.

Scott took the snap and ran down the middle, cut to the left to dodge a linebacker, and sprinted up the sideline 70 yards as time expired, giving Wood River a 27-0 halftime lead, burying the Bluejays.

"We were disappointed at halftime," Ravenna coach Keith Albright said afterward.

But the game that solidified Scott as a bona fide college prospect, the one that put him on the path to one of the best high school careers in state history, came Nov. 6, 1990, an hour north of Wood River in Albion.

Larry's and Carol's offense wasn't working in the first half. The low point came when Scott threw a poor pass at the 1-yard line that was returned 99 yards for a touchdown. The Eagles trailed 26-7 at the half.

"And then," Gideon said, "Scott just took over."

In the second half, in the span of eight minutes, Scott scored on touchdown runs of 50, 45 and 34 yards and blocked a punt, all while sniffing out Albion runs from his linebacker position.

The Eagles rallied and won 35-26, advancing in the C-1 playoffs.

"That's when he became a man on the football field, just took over mentally and physically," Gideon said.

Wood River was knocked out of the playoffs the following week, but after a 10-2 season, Scott's name further spread around the state. The sophomore finished the year with 1,850 passing yards and 18 touchdowns. On the ground, he had 954 yards and 16 touchdowns. He added 97 tackles and seven interceptions on defense.

He was named Class C-1 All-State as a defensive back by The World-Herald.

USA Today put Scott on its Faces to Watch list for the high school sports season in January 1991.

And by the fall of 1991, more faces would show up to see who this kid from Wood River really was.

DINNER CONVERSATION AT the Frost table was filled with talk about sports.

"Poor kids," Larry said. "Athletics have been our life. We've not pushed them, but pulled them along."

The Frosts lived and breathed football. It was their life, especially in those four years with Scott as quarterback in Wood River. And the foundation Carol and Larry set for their sons no doubt had an impact on Scott's later decision to coach. Particularly influential was his mother. With an optimistic outlook and a history of breaking gender barriers, there were not many things that would deter her once she set her mind to it.

Carol was not the first paid female football coach in Nebraska, but when hired at McCook in 1986 by her husband, she became the first in the state since World War II.

In the early 1980s, when the Frosts lived in O'Neill, Nebraska, Larry didn't have enough coaches for the football team. The superintendent of the school suggested asking Carol to coach. She taught math at O'Neill.

"I thought I would be run out of town," Larry said.

But he asked his wife, and she obliged, flinging passes and coaching up the receivers.

"That first year went very well," Larry said. "The kids and parents didn't seem to have any problems."

Carol did the same job a few years later in Palestine, Texas, where Carol would later recall some doubting dads showing up for one of the first practices. Doubt was erased when the men realized the coach's wife could throw harder and more accurately than any of them.

Only once does Larry recall an issue with an opposing coach. It came in Texas when Palestine played Jacksonville. A coach from Jacksonville said something to one of Carol's receivers.

"We ended up throwing for 205 yards and two touchdowns," Larry said. "We beat them 17-0. Our whole group of receivers headed for that coach right after the game. He turned tail and ran. Rather than being embarrassed, the kids were really proud that Carol was their coach."

At Wood River, Carol was paid to coach receivers and defensive ends. On the first day of practice in 1989, the skeptics were out again, including Gideon.

Carol started throwing long "out" passes to the receivers, a skill she had honed back in the late 1960s when she used to throw to Larry while he was with Nebraska.

"She could literally throw the ball as hard as Scott," Gideon remembers. "She would do all the drills, and yeah, it wasn't an underhand toss. It was a perfect throwing motion."

Carol sat in the press box during games. Using their headsets, Larry would call a play, and Carol would give input. This system of play-calling is what Scott would later use as head coach at Central Florida.

But perhaps what Carol did better than anything was connect with her players. She and Larry made a point to get to know their guys, to build up their players team, rather than tear them down.

No doubt, Gideon said, sometimes father and quarterback got in shouting matches at practice. But Larry and Carol — Carol especially — went out of their way to build team harmony.

"Larry and Carol just had an unbelievable ability to get the most of every kid, and made them believe in themselves," Gideon said. "That was a great quality."

Years later, this mantra was also adopted by Scott, particularly at Central Florida. When the team broke down practice at UCF, a coach would yell, "one team," and the team would yell back, "one heartbeat." The Wood River teams, Gideon said, were exceptionally close, in part because of how Carol tried to connect with the players and the culture the Frosts tried to build.

"To me, she's a perfect assistant," Larry said of Carol in 1986. "... She is very patient and understands technique. You have to know the value of technique when you weigh only 140 pounds and still become the national discus champion."

Her other duty, for both the team and for Scott, was to monitor the family phone. After Scott's sophomore season, Division I coaches started asking around for the Frosts' phone number.

After that 1991 season, the phone began to ring. And soon, it wouldn't stop.

MATT GIDEON WAS A HUNTER.

He loved being on the river, waiting for whitetail deer and watching sunrises on cold mornings, with warm coffee in his hand.

He daydreamed about it often.

On that freezing November night in 1991, Scott looked over and didn't like the look on Gideon's face. Especially not right now, in the fourth quarter.

"Matt!" Scott yelled from his linebacker position.

Gideon, out at cornerback, looked over.

"Quit thinking about hunting deer and get your head in the game!"

Gideon tried to protest, but before he could explain himself, St. Cecilia was running another play, this time from the 1-yard line. The running back barreled through the line and bumped into the end zone.

The score: 19-19, with 5:03 remaining.

St. Cecilia lined up for the extra point. Scott, furious, took his place on the right side of the line.

The ball was snapped, the hold was good but Scott slipped past the defensive end, dove and smacked the extra point away, his second block of an extra point in the game. Fans in the bleachers and around the track erupted.

It was the type of play Wood River fans grew to expect from Scott in 1991, during what, at the time, was the greatest season in school history.

Every game night in Wood River, it was the Scott Frost show.

In Week Two against Loup City, Scott scored five touchdowns, racked up 330 yards of offense, averaged 25.4 yards per carry and returned a punt 60 yards. He scored a touchdown every fourth time he ran or threw the ball.

Two weeks later against Burwell, Scott threw for 207 yards and a touchdown and ran for 93 yards and two scores. In the second quarter, he returned a punt 55 yards for another score. And just before half, Scott picked off a pass over the middle in the end zone, shed three tackles near the goal line and took off for a 105-yard interception return. That score remains the longest touchdown in Nebraska prep history.

"We were in the ball game," Burwell coach Tim Hurlburt said afterward. "There were just two big plays we didn't have much control over."

By Week Six, Scott surpassed 1,000 passing yards and 1,000 rushing yards.

The Wood River offense was a machine. Against St. Cecilia during the regular season in Game Seven, the Eagles rolled up 566 yards of total offense in an easy 54-12 win.

Oct. 11, 1991: Wood River vs. Hastings St. Cecilia in the regular season.

In Larry's up-tempo, option-based system, which he learned from Bob Devaney during his playing days at Nebraska, Wood River averaged 480 yards of total offense and usually ran around 80 plays.

Behind Scott in the backfield was Mike Gall, a junior fullback. Gall was a newcomer to the team but not to the Frost family. The boys grew up together in O'Neill, where their fathers coached. They played football in Palestine, where their fathers continued as coaching colleagues. The Gall family rejoined the Frosts before the start of the 1991 season. "They do make a really good team together," Larry said in 1991. "We work very hard at being as versatile as we can be. What Mike gives us is an inside threat."

Scott also had a host of receivers, including Gideon, senior Mark Codner and an offensive line that moved defenders like a snow plow moves snowflakes. Wood River's center that year, Gerrod Lambrecht, would later become Scott's chief of staff at Nebraska.

By Week 10, Scott was averaging 314.1 yards of total offense per game, a pace that would have ranked fifth on the all-time national list at the time.

All that led to the 7-2 record and this playoff rematch with St. Cecilia, now tied at 19 heading into overtime.

St. Cecilia won the toss and chose to give Wood River the ball first. Then as now, high school overtime rules give both teams the ball at the 10-yard line.

Scott took over and the Eagles ran on first, second and third down. In the first half, that strategy yielded 202 yards of offense. But in overtime, the Eagles gained just 1 yard on the three run plays.

On fourth down from the 9-yard line, Scott dropped back to throw. Gideon, split to the right, ran into the end zone, planted, turned and lost his defender. Scott threw a bullet on the run to Gideon, who caught his sixth pass of the day to give

Wood River a 26-19 lead with Brandon Bayley's extra-point kick.

St. Cecilia took over and scored immediately. Quarterback J.L. Vertin found tight end Scott Schriner alone in the end zone when Wood River bit hard on a first down play-action run.

26-25.

It was decision time for St. Cecilia coach Carl Tesmer. Kick the extra point and risk it being blocked — remember, Scott had already blocked two kicks — or go for two.

Tesmer sent his offense back onto the field to go for the win.

Fans in the bleachers stood. The four rows of people on the track huddled closer. This was it.

Vertin took the snap and handed to powerful running back Kory Bumgardner, who was met at the line by Wood River linebacker Lance Parlin. Scott and the front seven climbed onto the pile and pushed St. Cecilia backwards. And for the first time in years, Wood River was advancing in the state playoffs.

It's a game, years later, Wood River fans still remember. For Scott's pass, for the blocked extra points, for the goal-line stand.

The Eagles lost 49-6 the next week to powerhouse Battle Creek, not scoring on the eventual state runner-up until the game's final 58 seconds, but the season was considered a success at 8-3.

Scott finished the year averaging 311.6 yards of offense per game, good for sixth all-time nationally. He passed for 1,964 yards and ran for 1,464. He scored 39 touchdowns — 17 passing, 19 rushing, two kick returns and that 105-yard interception return. He was honored by The World-Herald as the first-team All-Nebraska quarterback.

More than ever, college coaches around the country took notice.

Scott, with the ball, eyes the defense in the first round of the 1991 Class C-1 playoffs against Hastings St. Cecilia. Later in the game, he blocks what would have been a game-winning extra point and then hits Matt Gideon in the end zone to give Wood River a 26-25 overtime win.

Scott finishes his 1991 high school junior season as one the top quarterbacks in the country. He averages 311.6 yards of offense, good for sixth all-time nationally. He passes for 1,964 yards and runs for 1,464 yards. He scores 39 touchdowns, including two kick returns and a 105-yard interception return. With a year left, Frost has more than 7,300 yards of total offense.

JULY 15, 1992

PRIZE QB PUTS TOWN ON MAP

BY TOM SHATEL

Memo: To Tom Osborne, Bobby Bowden, Bill Walsh and Lou Holtz.

Re: Directions to the next great college quarterback.

Gentlemen: Take Interstate 80, get off on exit 300 and head south. Go over two Platte River bridges. Loop around a 90-degree curve to the left. Get to another curve, only head left instead down a gravel road for about a half-mile. The Frost house sits by itself, on the right. Finding Scott Frost figures to be easier than landing him.

As you sit on a couch in the Frost house, with proud parents Larry and Carol discussing their All-American kid, it's easy to picture Stanford Head Football Coach Walsh or Notre Dame's Holtz in this very living room next winter. Getting there is another image. I'd pay to see the great Walsh negotiate his way down that gravel road on a cold Nebraska night. Just look for the "No hunting or fishing" sign, Bill.

That is next January. Now, all is quiet around Scott Frost. And all is perfect. The summer before your senior year is full of anticipation. That goes double for Frost, a 6-foot-3, 200-pound, blond-haired bundle of dreams who, for the world, looks like a young John Elway.

With Elwayesque expectations.

Frost is looking at a year in which he should lead his Wood River team on a run toward the Class C-1 state title, polish academic skills that already have produced an ACT score of 29 and make the decision of his life: Which university he will use as his catapult to fame and fortune.

Meanwhile, excuse him while he goes out to feed the cows.

Ah, the glamorous life of a high-school phenom. Frost is in hog heaven, though, working on a farm just north of Wood River. When he's not tending to livestock and irrigating corn, his "vacations" are trips to summer football camps. Frost, who already has attended Nebraska, Notre Dame and Wyoming camps this summer, is getting tips from Bowden at Florida State this week.

That's how you spend the summer before your big year. Are we having fun yet?

"It's fun," Scott says, "but it's a lot of work, too."

Work?

"Camp is like having three-a-days," Scott said. "You have two practices during the day, then you have to study plays and practice again at night. You don't get a lot of rest."

Camps are a necessity but you get plenty of exposure and, if you're Scott Frost, early scholarship offers. Frost said he already has offers from Iowa, Colorado State and Fresno State, with some pretty strong hinting by Osborne at Nebraska and Notre Dame's Holtz, who told Frost, "I plan on coaching you."

Frost's coach this year will continue to be his father, Larry, the Wood River head coach who gladly pays summer-camp expenses for the extra fundamental work and exposure for his star quarterback.

"If you come from Wood River or anywhere in Nebraska, you probably need the exposure, so these camps become a necessity," Larry Frost said. "Nebraska has seen him, but Notre Dame, Florida State and BYU are witnessing him for the first time. It does help. They're good investments."

Even if they haven't actually seen it, though, most colleges have heard of the young gun from Wood River.

Recruiting coordinators from Nebraska, Colorado, Texas, BYU, Stanford, Air Force, Colorado State, Kansas State and Wyoming visited Frost in Wood River this spring. To be sure, these reconnaissance missions were to scout out the player and the territory, gravel roads and all.

What recruiters will find this year, however, is a kid with the deepest of Nebraska roots.

Scott was born in Lincoln. His father grew up in Malcolm, Neb. -- "seven miles from Memorial Stadium" -- and later was a wingback on Bob Devaney's 1968 and 1969 Nebraska teams. He then began a Nebraska high school coaching trek through Crete, Lincoln, O'Neill, McCook and Wood River (with a four-year stop in Texas). Carol, from Cedar Rapids, Neb., also attended NU, is a former Nebraska women's track coach and threw the discus for the United States in the 1968 Summer Olympic Games.

"Athletics has been our whole life," Larry said. "We (he and Carol) met on a track. We've both been coaches. They (their sons) didn't have much of a chance to do anything else. I don't know if we pushed them into sports. We probably pulled them along."

Rounding out Team Frost is Steve, a sophomore offensive lineman at Colorado State and model for the Scott Frost recruiting process.

"Looking back at when he was recruited, I'm not sure I did a good enough job, as his coach, of selling him to schools," Larry said. "I wish I would have sent more films out on him. I'll do that with Scott."

One thing Coach Frost will do for his son is help cut down a list of "a half-dozen" schools before the season starts in September. That's easier said than done. Asked for a list of schools he wants to consider, Scott said: "Washington, Stanford, Colorado, Colorado State, Notre Dame, Michigan, Nebraska, Kansas State, Notre Dame, Florida State and BYU."

And though he "grew up" a Nebraska fan, the kid says he's now "a fan of football." Translation: Nebraska is anything but a lock. Frost, who threw for 1,900 yards and ran for 1,400 last year in a veer offense, wants to go where he can air it out and also run some option. Mostly, he wants to play, which would put NU in a precarious position because of freshman quarterbacks Tony Veland and Tommie Frazier.

"I really haven't had too much pressure to stay in state," Scott said. "Most of the kids get excited when they hear Michigan or Notre Dame or BYU. The grown-ups are the ones who talk about going to Nebraska."

All but two grown-ups, that is. Larry and Carol, NU roots and all, are staying out of it. Except for when Osborne comes to visit.

"He was my position coach," Larry said. "Next winter, we'll sit down and say, 'You've seen Scott play this year and now you've seen Veland and Frazier play so give us an honest assessment of whether Scott will play or not.' And knowing Coach Osborne, that's what we'll get. I, for one, will believe it."

Osborne impressed at the NU camp by personally tutoring the quarterbacks, something other head coaches, Frost says, didn't do. But the biggest impression came in South Bend, where former Irish quarterback Tom Clements is the offensive coordinator.

"Coach Clements gave us three of their pass plays and showed us how to read pass coverages on the plays," Frost said. "Then they cut up some film and showed their quarterbacks doing the same plays in games last year, and we were able to see if they made the right read or not. I enjoyed that. That really helped."

It's something to use this fall at Wood River. And it's on Frost's brain most of these long summer days.

"I'm excited about it," Frost said. "This is my last year, and I hope it's my best. I'm working (on the farm) with one of my teammates, and we talk about it all the time; how we're going to do, what it's going to take. We can't wait to get started."

But what about the having fun part?

"With success comes fun," said Carol Frost, the Wood River boys track coach last season. "Winning football games and keeping your grades up is what makes for fun around our house."

That's what you do on your summer vacation in a house of coaches. You keep your dreams in perspective.

"It's not a matter of him getting a scholarship - he will," Larry said. "He has to focus on this year and having a great season. If you do that, everything else will take care of itself."

Just the same, they might want to start working on a map. There are a lot of gravel roads out here.

SCOTT ENTERS HIS SENIOR YEAR AS A TOP QUARTERBACK PROSPECT, AND COLLEGE COACHES FROM ACROSS THE COUNTRY SEEK HIM OUT. "HE HAS TO FOCUS ON THIS YEAR AND HAVING A GREAT SEASON," SAID HIS DAD AND COACH IN JULY 1992. "IF YOU DO THAT, EVERYTHING ELSE WILL TAKE CARE OF ITSELF."

FROST ATTRACTS EYES OF NATION

OMAHA WORLD-HERALD

Not even Nebraska I-back Calvin Jones, while at Omaha Central, received the national attention being given to Wood River quarterback Scott Frost.

At halftime of tonight's home game against Kearney Catholic, Frost will receive the first Old Spice Athlete of the Month national award. His presenter will be former NU All-America quarterback Jerry Tagge. Frost has yet to play a fourth quarter in Wood River's 2-0 start. Last week he threw for 214 yards and four touchdowns, ran for 94 yards and a touchdown and scored a sixth touchdown on a 78-yard interception return.

"That might have been one of the best games Scott's had," said his father, Wood River Coach Larry Frost.

Old Spice announced Scott Frost's selection in the Sept. 7 issue of Sports Illustrated.

All-America Nebraska quarterback Jerry Tagge — a former teammate of Scott's dad, Larry — presents a national athlete of the month award to Scott.

THE MAGAZINE LANDED in Nebraska mailboxes on Sept. 3, 1992.

Sports Illustrated's cover boy was Jerry Rice, but tucked among feature stories about British lawn-mower races and how computers were transforming coaching strategy, between ads for Gameboy and Motorola's two-way radios, readers found a full-page promotion for the Old Spice athlete of the month.

The headline: "Frosty the Showman."

The Wood River (Neb.) Eagles trailed Albion High 26-7 late in the third quarter last season. The game would have been out of reach except for a quarterback who says, "I really don't like to lose." In the next eight minutes, 6'3", 205-pound Scott Frost put on an incredible show, scoring on touchdown runs of 50, 45 and 34 yards and blocking a punt as the Eagles won 35-26. Exploits like these make the 17-year-old high school senior the first Old Spice Athlete of the Month.

"To this day," Larry said, "we don't understand why they took him out of the thousands they could have. We all thought the ad was very well done. One of the nice things from it is that we've received a ton of letters from people we've known across the country whom we haven't seen for a long time."

The publicity, and the recruitment, of Scott was becoming national. And it was picking up steam.

The next four months after the magazine published was one of the most intense recruiting battles in Nebraska high school history. Stanford coach Bill Walsh got lost on the way to the Grand Island airport. Osborne called the Frost house seven times one night. Devaney, the godfather of Nebraska football, even stepped in late for a Hail Mary.

All told, Scott received about 3,000 pieces of mail. A few letters even wished him the worst, perhaps a sign that all the publicity was wearing thin in some corners of the state.

"It's hard for me to believe that anyone can be that interested in where my life goes," Scott said in January 1993.

It all goes with the territory when you make as much noise as Scott already had heading into his senior season.

He was about to shatter the state record for total yards of offense. And in a state that prides itself on in-state recruiting, Scott's presence in Wood River was a beacon of hope for the continued success of Husker football.

By August 1992, Scott had scholarship offers from Nebraska, Colorado State, BYU, Fresno State, Notre Dame, Colorado, Wyoming, Arizona State and Washington.

It was Colorado, a Nebraska nemesis, that had an early lead for Scott's services.

The first two weeks of Wood River's season, Scott loaded up his car after games and headed west. On Sept. 6, 1992, he played half a game, throwing for 96 yards and rushing for 106 yards on 11 carries in Wood River's first win. He then trekked to Boulder to visit the University of Colorado. The following weekend, just hours after throwing four touchdown passes, running for a score and returning an interception 78 yards for a touchdown, Scott drove to Fort Collins to visit his brother, Steve, at Colorado State.

Being close to Steve, Scott thought, would be a nice asset for college.

Old Spice flew to Wood River for Game Three to present Scott with the Athlete of the Month Award. Former Husker quarterback Jerry Tagge handed Scott the award at halftime.

By October of Scott's senior season, the scene Gideon was so taken aback by a year prior had become the norm. On Homecoming night, Oct. 10, 1992, 2,300 fans crowded the bleachers and track for Wood River's 47-20 victory over St. Cecilia. Scott had a hand in six touchdowns, two by running and four by passing, with 281 total yards of offense.

"Frost did his thing," St. Cecilia Coach Carl Tesmer said after the game. "He's a lot better than last year."

By that point in the season, Scott had already broken the all-time record for total yards in a career by a high school athlete in Nebraska, with a little more than 6,000.

Four days after that game, Nebraska recruiting coordinator Dave Gillespie all but said Nebraska was setting its sights on Scott Frost, despite having a crowded quarterback depth chart.

"If there were a great quarterback out there who wanted to come, we would encourage him to do so," Gillespie said, unable to acknowledge Scott by name due to NCAA rules.

Scott's season rolled on, and as it did, the phone calls increased. Sometimes as many as five a night from Division I coaches, including from Walsh at Stanford, Holtz at Notre Dame and Osborne.

Eventually, the Frosts had to buy an answering machine.

"It was kind of like being in a state fair for 10 to 12 weeks," Larry said.

In general, Scott was grateful for the recruitment, but at times it grew tiring.

"Some of the coaches ... are pretty full of it," Scott said in 1993. "They'd talk about the weather or ask about your girlfriend."

One night, Scott's stomach was growling as he listened to a long-winded coach. He set the phone down, went to the kitchen and got a Little Debbie snack cake.

"When I came back, he was still talking," Scott said. "I didn't miss a thing."

SEPT. 6, 1992

WOOD RIVER BEATS CAIRO CENTURA 60-8.

OMAHA WORLD-HERALD

Scott Frost needs about 2,700 yards in total offense this season to move into second place on the national all-time leader list. Scott exceeded that total in his sophomore and junior seasons. "He has an outside chance to become the all-time total offense leader, and second place is definitely within reach," Larry Frost said.

Around that time, Scott was becoming aware of the pressures put upon a top quarterback recruit, particularly in Nebraska.

"You have to do the right things all the time with people watching you," he said. "I'd be lying if I said the stress and jealousy didn't get to me."

In the final game of the regular season, Scott ran for 168 yards and passed for 215 in Wood River's 36-7 win over previously unbeaten Adams Central. In that game, Scott became only the third high school player in history nationally to reach 10,000 yards of total offense.

As Scott's fame grew, friends were sure to try to keep his ego in check.

"If he ever got a big head, we'd hit him hard," said longtime friend Gall.

"We all know he's a great player," Lambrecht said at the time. "Any press he gets brings attention to the team. To play with him is an honor. But we're never afraid to put him in his place."

Entering the playoffs, Wood River was averaging 50.3 points per game, just five points shy of the state record, which was 55.7 set by Taylor in 1950. Most of the starters were seniors who'd grown into Larry's and Carol's up-tempo offense. Confidence in winning a state title was high.

"We have four real good running backs that Dad's not afraid to give the ball to," Scott said at the time. "Our receivers aren't speedsters, but they run great patterns, find the ball and do a great job."

Eventually, Wood River and Battle Creek found themselves facing each other in the C-1 playoffs for the second season in a row.

While Wood River was just getting a taste of success, Battle Creek was a dynasty from the northeast. Battle Creek had one of the state's coaching legends, Bob Schnitzler, whose teams

won 293 games for him before he retired. Four teams won state titles, another five were in state finals.

Battle Creek also had the players to keep up with Wood River. That year's Omaha World-Herald All-Nebraska team included three Braves — offensive tackle Jay Korth, linebacker Matt Hoskinson and I-back Todd Uhlir — still the most ever for a Class C-1 school. Uhlir's 2,849 yards that season and 5,926 in his career set state records. Hoskinson went on to be a top backup at offensive guard, blocking for Frost, on NU's 1996 and 1997 teams, and Korth was all-conference at Wyoming.

The rematch with Battle Creek, this time on the Braves' turf before 4,000 fans from all over northeast Nebraska, was more competitive than the year prior. At half, Battle Creek led, 37-20.

The Braves wore down Wood River by rushing for a C-1 playoff record 525 yards. Uhlir ran for 310 yards, five touchdowns and four two-point conversions. Scott threw for 191 yards and ran for 106 yards, scoring three touchdowns.

It wasn't near enough. The Eagles lost, 67-26.

The score was so shocking to those around Wood River and the south central part of the state that the television station in Hastings temporarily reported the score inaccurately, believing there was no way Wood River could suffer such a lop-sided loss.

Scott finished his career with 11,095 total yards, third highest all-time nationally and double the previous Nebraska state record.

In total, Scott accounted for 146 touchdowns in high school and finished 33-11 in four years as the Wood River quarterback. Again, he was The World-Herald's All-Nebraska quarterback.

But that era was now over.

It was time to pick a college.

WOOD RIVER HIGH SCHOOL: 1989-1992
#7 SCOTT FROST

	PASS YARDS	PASS TDS	RUSH YARDS	RUSH TDS
1989	837	11	275	18
1990	1,850	18	954	16
1991	1,964	17	1,464	19
1992	2,142	21	1,585	26

ONE OF THE MOST
HIGHLY RECRUITED
ATHLETES IN THE
NATION IN 1993.
DIVISION 1
SCHOLARSHIP
OFFERS FROM:

- Nebraska
- Stanford
- Colorado State
- Brigham Young
- Fresno State
- Notre Dame
- Colorado
- Wyoming
- Arizona State
- Washington

▼ NEBRASKA ALL-CLASS RECORDS

MOST CAREER YARDS	MOST SINGLE-SEASON YARDS	MOST CAREER TOUCHDOWNS	LONGEST INTERCEPTION-RETURN TOUCHDOWN
11,095	3,727 IN 1992	152 79 RUSH, 67 PASS, SIX RETURNS	105-YARDS VS BURWELL SEPT. 30, 1991

MOST CAREER PASSING YARDS	MOST CAREER TOUCHDOWN PASSES	MOST COMPLETIONS	YARDS PER-GAME AVERAGE
6,793	67	447	311.6 IN 1991

▲ CLASS C-1 RECORDS

ONE DAY, IN THE WINTER of 1992, Scott walked into Elizabeth Hodtwalker's room at Wood River High.

He needed some help.

He was going to be giving a speech soon, a press conference to announce his college choice. And he wanted to do it right.

Hodtwalker taught him Spanish at Wood River. Even directed him in two one-act school plays.

Of course, she said. She'd help.

And over the next few weeks, she met with the All-American quarterback after school to talk about posture. About tone. About what questions not to answer.

In the meantime, Scott's legend was growing far beyond the state's borders. The Tampa Tribune ranked him as the No. 9 overall recruit in the 1993 recruiting class. Tom Lemming, a leading national recruiting guru, ranked him the No. 11 overall player.

Scott whittled his offers to Stanford and Nebraska. He visited Notre Dame but didn't particularly like what Holtz was selling, and he'd long since decided to pass on Colorado.

And so it was Nebraska, where he'd always dreamed of playing, or Stanford, where he could be coached by three-time Super Bowl champion and former San Francisco 49ers head coach Bill Walsh. Scott was torn. There was the school he'd grown up in, literally, playing in the shot put circle on the Nebraska track as a toddler while his mom coached the track team, or a school he thought would be a better path to play quarterback in the NFL.

"He has aspirations, realistic or not, of making a living playing football, and if he's going to stay as a quarterback, you wonder if he shouldn't go somewhere that runs a pro-style offense," Larry told a local TV station.

The first time Walsh visited Wood River, he walked into the gym during basketball practice. The action stopped, head basketball coach Dale Smidt said.

"It's the most different thing I've been through," said Smidt in 1992. He'd been a resident of Wood River for 30 years at the time. "It threw the whole town into a tizzy, without a doubt."

Scott, who averaged 16 points on the basketball court and was eventually named second team Class C-1 all-state, left with Walsh after practice and took him to the usual spot: Dowd's restaurant in nearby Alda.

The pitch from Walsh was always pretty simple: Come to Stanford, be the next Joe Montana.

That name, Joe Montana, kept coming up between Scott and Walsh.

At that time, Montana was with the Kansas City Chiefs on the downward leg of his career. But Montana was revered; even a legend to many: four-time Super Bowl champion, three-time Super Bowl MVP, eight-time Pro Bowler, two-time NFL regular season MVP, 1990 Sports Illustrated Sportsman of the Year. For Scott, the idea of being coached by the man who coached Montana was a dream.

After dinner, Walsh headed back to the airport, but actually got lost on the Nebraska highways.

"He got lost going to the airport in Grand Island," Scott said in 1992. "He was staying at a hotel on the interstate, and all he had to do was take Highway 281 to the airport. He ended up in someplace like St. Paul, and he was pretty upset about it."

Lost, maybe, but Walsh had found his way inside Scott's head. The Nebraska boy, the son of two Nebraska athletes, started to really consider leaving.

Despite ties to Nebraska, there were practical matters that seemed to stand in the way. The Huskers were loaded at the quarterback position. Nebraska had four scholarship quarterbacks with eligibility left after the 1992 season: Tommie Frazier, who started the final seven games of his true freshman season; redshirt freshmen Tony Veland and Brook Berringer and incoming freshman Ben Rutz.

But even so, Nebraska wasn't about to let another school come in and steal an in-state talent like Scott without a fight.

"We're going to try and recruit Scott Frost, without a doubt," quarterbacks coach Turner Gill said. "He's a great quarterback and a great athlete."

The Frosts and Nebraska obviously went way back. Osborne had recruited Larry, and the family knew nearly everything there was to know about the school and football program. So Scott chose to use his five official visits elsewhere.

Including to Stanford.

The weekend before Christmas, Scott took his official visit to the Bay Area. He visited Walsh's house, where he received an unexpected present: a meeting with Joe Montana.

Technically, it was a recruiting violation — the NCAA later investigated. Walsh said the meeting was by accident, as did the Frosts. Violation or not, here was Frost, shaking hands with Montana, who was offering to take Frost to the practice fields to throw passes to Jerry Rice.

The meeting undoubtedly helped Walsh make his case.

Plus, Stanford's depth at quarterback wasn't nearly as deep as Nebraska's. When discussing playing time, Walsh even brought Montana into that sales pitch, saying with the 49ers, Steve DeBerg was the quarterback during Montana's first year, but they added packages just for Montana so he could get some experience.

The plan was to do the same with Scott and returning Stanford starter Steve Stenstrom.

Scott returned to Wood River with even more reasons to leave his home state. Carol was on Team Stanford, Larry on Team Nebraska. Scott was still somewhere in between.

After the Stanford visit, Osborne invited Scott to Lincoln for two days in mid-January.

HIGH SCHOOL AWARDS

- Omaha World-Herald Male Athlete of the Year
- Two-time Nebraska Offensive Player of the Year
- First-Team All-State in football for three seasons
- Honorary captain of the All-Nebraska football team
- Named a high school All-American by ESPN and Parade magazine in 1992
- Honorable Mention All-America by USA Today
- Gatorade's Central Regional football player of the year in 1992
- Second-Team Class C-1 in basketball, averaging 16 points
- All-class gold in the shot put with a heave of 58-9½ (1993)
- C-1 champion in the 110 high hurdles and runner-up for all-class gold (1993)
- Three-time Academic All-State

The Wood River Eagles football seniors gather around Scott and display their four years of awards and mementos.

All day on Jan. 16 and 17 in Lincoln, Scott talked with Osborne, Gill and Frank Solich. His main worry was playing time, and Nebraska's plan for him, Frazier and Rutz.

"Tommie did a great job this year, and the state and media are behind him," Scott said. "It would be tough to unseat him. But I think Osborne would play whoever he thinks is best."

The talks helped Scott, and the argument from the coaching staff was, essentially, Frost's fit at Nebraska was too perfect to let slip away. After those two days of talks, Frost said he needed a few days to think. Not only had Nebraska given him compelling reasons to stay, but there was a new element thrown into the mix: his brother.

Steve was leaving Colorado State and had two scholarship offers:

Nebraska and Stanford.

A package deal?

"Both schools insisted it wasn't," Larry said. "But, my goodness, for Mom and Dad, what a wonderful thing it would be to have them both together. They may end up being the first center-quarterback brother combination in Nebraska history, who knows?"

Over the next two weeks, Scott fielded calls from Walsh and was visited at school by Solich and another NU assistant, Dan Young. Nebraska fans started writing letters to encourage Scott to commit. Some even got hold of the family's phone number and began calling at night.

"Everybody was really nice," Scott said. "Most congratulated me on what I accomplished. People said they hoped to see me at Nebraska, but they wished me luck with wherever I go."

Maybe the biggest phone call, though, came from Bob Devaney — the legendary Husker coach who jumpstarted Nebraska football by winning 101 out of 123 games from 1962 to 1972 and winning two national titles. He called the house one night and gave Scott one final pitch.

Scott talks at a press conference to announce his decision to attend Stanford.

By late January, Scott came to a decision. Armed with Mrs. Hodtwalker's tips about tone and ways to tone down arrogance, he called a press conference at Wood River High School.

He had an announcement to make.

Almost apologetically, Scott announced he'd be leaving his home state to play college football at Stanford.

"The opportunity to play in a pro-style offense under Bill Walsh at an institution as prestigious as Stanford was more than I felt I could pass up," Scott said. "I hope the test of time will prove this to be a wise decision."

Frost's choice divided the state. And the family. Larry was crushed, particularly since he had to call Devaney and tell him his son was going elsewhere.

"That's going to be the toughest thing for me," Larry said on national signing day. "Bob Devaney means so much to our family."

Wood River, in general, wasn't all that thrilled. Husker fans felt betrayed. Those closest to Scott, though, seemed to understand, particularly when Scott broke it down to them in person.

"We knew what he was dreaming of, what he was trying to do, and you really couldn't blame him for what he did," Gideon said.

Scott's main worry wasn't criticism, but his future of living in a different state. But on the same day Scott made his decision public, Steve announced he'd be leaving Colorado State to transfer to Stanford, which Scott believed would make things better.

Maybe happiest of all on signing day was Walsh.

"Scott has the potential to be a truly great college player, and ultimately a truly great professional quarterback," Walsh said. "We're on the cutting edge of offensive football, especially for the quarterback position."

Nebraska coaches, on the other hand, were stung.

Before the press conference, Scott called the Nebraska football office to talk to a coach, but no one was in. So he told a secretary of his decision and to pass it along to a coach when she had a chance.

"I'm sure they'll be calling tonight," he said. "I'm sure they'll be disappointed. In a lot of ways, I'm disappointed I'm not going to get to go down there and play before my home state. I've been torn through all of this. They've already got great quarterbacks. They've got a great team, and I'm sure their program will go on without me."

Said Osborne on signing day: "We felt badly about missing on Scott Frost. He's a very good player. We've known him and his brother since they were little children, so we hated to miss on that one."

> "WE FELT BADLY ABOUT MISSING ON SCOTT FROST. HE'S A VERY GOOD PLAYER. WE'VE KNOWN HIM AND HIS BROTHER SINCE THEY WERE LITTLE CHILDREN, SO WE HATED TO MISS ON THAT ONE."
> — TOM OSBORNE ON SIGNING DAY IN 1993

But Nebraska had to move on. And so did Scott.

He played basketball that winter. He won all-class gold in the shot put and Class C gold in the 110 hurdles. Like his father, Larry, before him, Scott played in the Nebraska Shrine Bowl.

Just weeks before leaving for college, Scott was still holding onto his Nebraska fandom.

Gideon had a copy of the Nebraska-Miami 1984 Orange Bowl on VHS, and as school winded down in the spring, Gideon would fire up the VCR and he and Scott would watch the game over and over.

They'd watch Osborne bypass the tie and go for two against Miami for the national title. They'd grimace as the Miami pass rush closed in on Gill. Their hearts would sink as Gill's pass to Jeff Smith was batted away.

Despite plans to leave the state and play for another program, something was telling Scott his Nebraska journey may not be over.

"Hopefully things will work out at Stanford as quarterback. If not, I suppose I could switch positions or go to another college," Scott said at his signing day press conference.

"Probably Nebraska."

BIG CROWD STAYS TO SEE FROST WIN ALL-CLASS GOLD

BY STU POSPISIL

Scott Frost was by himself Friday. In front of a lot of people.

The Wood River senior won the all-class gold medal in the boys shot put as the last competitor in Class C. His final three attempts were delayed so he could run in the preliminaries for the 300-meter intermediate hurdles.

When he returned to the shot-put area northeast of Burke Stadium, more than 300 people lined the storm fences to see the Stanford football recruit aim for a gold medal he had long wanted.

He got it on his final attempt with a heave of 58 feet, 9½ inches.

"We've walked this grass for three years," said his mother, Wood River Coach Carol Frost, "seeing if we could finally win an all-class gold.

"But the timing was the worst."

Frost returned for the final three attempts with the Class C title in hand. He had a 56-7½ in the preliminaries.

But on the board was the 57-2 by Class A champion Lincoln Southeast's Eric Anderson. Frost and Anderson were the honorary captains of The World-Herald All-Nebraska football team.

Frost's first attempt in the finals traveled 55-5.

"Use your legs, Scott," his mother yelled.

Frost improved to 57-6½ and 58-9½ on his final attempts.

"I wish I could have gotten 60 again," he said. "Once I got the lead, it was a relief. It was easy to explode on the last one."

At the 1993 state track meet, Scott holds Class C's best qualifying time in the 110-meter high hurdles at 14.98 seconds. He also qualifies in the 300 hurdles with a time of 40.42.

Frost ranks seventh on the state's all-time list with a best of 61-1½.

He could win another Class C title today. He had Class C's best qualifying time in the 110-meter high hurdles, 14.98, and also qualified in the 300 hurdles, 40.42.

Frost said it was the first time he had to run the 300 hurdles, then complete his shot put attempts.

"I wish I had more time to get psyched for the hurdles," he said. "It's more mental to get ready than physical."

He said he was amazed that the crowd had waited around for more than a half-hour to watch him in the shot put.

"I couldn't believe it," he said. "I was expecting only a few fans would be there."

His parents, though, understood the commotion.

"He's gone through more scrutiny the past 12 months than anyone could imagine," said Larry Frost, Wood River's football coach.

Scott is the 1993 state champion in the shot put, winning the all-class gold medal with a throw of 58 feet, 9½ inches. His personal best from earlier that year was 61 feet, 1 inch. He beats Eric Anderson out of Lincoln Southeast who later serves as a 300-pound offensive lineman and starting right tackle at Nebraska with Frost. "Although he's not a big, bulky person," said Carol Frost, the mom and coach of the 6-foot-3, 215-pound Scott, "he's strong for his size."

1993 SHRINE BOWL

The 35th annual Shrine Bowl, July 31 at Memorial Stadium, is Scott's last high school game before heading to Stanford. Scott plays on the North squad coached by Ron Laux sharing quarterbacking duties with Millard North's Todd Doxzon (right). Playing about half the snaps, the game is not his best. While Scott accounts for the North's only touchdown with a 5-yard pass to tight end Josh Mc-Grane, he throws an interception on the last drive, sealing the South win, 12-7.

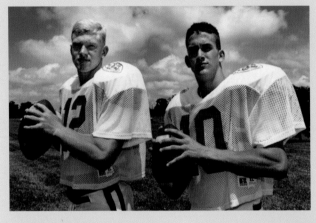

"IT WAS FRUSTRATING FOR ALL OF US AT TIMES. WE'RE ALL USED TO BEING IN THERE WHEN THE CHIPS ARE DOWN. ONLY HALF OF US COULD BE. I KNOW IT WAS FRUSTRATING FOR ME AND, I'M SURE IT WAS FOR DOXZON AND EVERYBODY ELSE WHO HAD TO SIT OUT."

— SCOTT FROST, SHRINE BOWL GAME

"YOU REALLY HAVE TO ADMIRE HIS DURABILITY. YOU CAN'T PUT THE STATS ON THE BOARD THE WAY HE DID FOR THREE OR FOUR YEARS BY HOBBLING AROUND. I THINK HE MISSED ONE BASKETBALL GAME AND ONE FOOTBALL GAME BECAUSE HE WAS HURT. AMAZING WHEN YOU CONSIDER THAT PEOPLE CERTAINLY KEYED ON HIM. HE HAD TREMENDOUS CONSISTENCY. AND HE SEEMED TO BE ABLE TO RISE TO THE OCCASION. HIS STATS WERE BETTER IN THE CLOSER OR TOUGHER GAMES."

— LARRY FROST AT THE END OF SCOTT'S HIGH SCHOOL SEASON

"IN FOOTBALL I FELT I HAD TO PROVE SOMETHING EVERY TIME I WENT ON THE FIELD. I WANTED TO SHOW THEM I WAS THE PLAYER THEY HAD HEARD ABOUT. I HAD TO DO A LOT OF GROWING UP THAT NORMAL TEENAGERS DON'T HAVE TO DO. WITH ALL OF THE ATTENTION, IT WAS TOUGH FOR ME. YOU HAVE TO DO THE RIGHT THINGS ALL THE TIME WITH PEOPLE WATCHING YOU. I'D BE LYING IF I SAID THE STRESS AND THE JEALOUSY DIDN'T GET TO ME. THE INTERVIEWS, THE PHONE CALLS GOT TO BE A HASSLE, BUT I KNOW THAT'S EXPECTED OF ANYONE IN THE NEWS. IT JUST HIT ME AT AN EARLIER AGE THAN IT DOES MOST PEOPLE."

— SCOTT, AFTER BEING NAMED THE OMAHA WORLD-HERALD'S MALE ATHLETE OF THE YEAR IN 1993

Tempe, Arizona, Sept. 21, 1996: Scott sits dejectedly in the end zone after a fourth-quarter safety against Arizona State. The Nebraska quarterback's second start ended in a 19-0 loss and the Huskers' first regular-season shutout since 1973.

FROM SHUTOUT TO STANDOUT

COLLEGE: 1993-1997

BY LEE BARFKNECHT

THIS ISN'T WHAT SCOTT FROST had in mind when he transferred from Stanford to Nebraska.

Not getting knocked on his can in the end zone at Arizona State for a safety — the third of the night, for God's sake — then firing the ball off the goal post in disgust during a 19-0 loss in his second start.

Not being the quarterback for the Huskers' first regular-season shutout since the Nixon administration (27-0 at Oklahoma in 1973).

Not twisting helplessly on the spit of criticism after completing 6 of 20 passes for 66 yards and rushing 10 times for minus-7 yards.

(Frost wasn't the only one who took a beating on that hot night in 1996. As World-Herald writers searched for a postgame beverage a few blocks from Sun Devil Stadium, Husker fans entered the hotel lobby disheveled and bug-eyed, reporting that anyone dressed in red wasn't safe from rowdy ASU fans celebrating revenge for a 77-28 loss at Nebraska a year earlier.)

No, this isn't what Frost envisioned at all after his time at Stanford — under offensive coaching icon Bill Walsh — produced a record of 7-14-1 with more starts at free safety than quarterback.

"I'm not going to say it was a bad decision to go to Stanford," Frost said entering the 1996 season at NU. "It just didn't turn out the way I wanted.

"After a year and a half, I wanted to be in a program that had a chance to win a national championship."

So he took over at quarterback for the preseason No. 1 team in the country, and two games later had to explain Nebraska's first loss in nearly 1,000 days.

Frost endured that, and much more, in his 2½ years at Nebraska, but eventually fulfilled his dream of helping NU claim a national championship in 1997.

The road Frost traveled to get to the top is worth a trip back in time.

Palo Alto, California, Sept. 17, 1994: As a Stanford Cardinal, Scott takes a snap during a game against San Jose State at Stanford Stadium.

"IT CAME DOWN TO Nebraska and Stanford," Frost said. "I made a decision at the time I thought was best. It was tough to leave the home state and friends and family. But it was something I wanted to try.

"I liked the pro-style offense, but it wasn't just football. I liked the education and I wanted to play for Bill Walsh."

So in 1993 off to the Bay Area of California went Frost and his brother, Steve, a lineman transferring from Colorado State in what was openly acknowledged as "a package deal" to play for an NFL champion head coach who invented the West Coast offense.

Playing time at quarterback wouldn't be automatic. Junior Steve Stenstrom was expected to start for a third straight season — and he did, as Frost worked to learn the offense from a playbook he referred to as "another Bible."

Frost played in all 11 games, but mostly as a change of pace on quarterback runs. His season statistics: 2 of 9 passes for six yards; 15 carries for 63 yards. No touchdowns in either category.

Stanford's record: 4-7. Frost's frustration level: Growing.

It climbed even more when Walsh asked him to add free safety to his resume for his second season while Stenstrom started again at quarterback. Walsh coated his request with plenty of syrup, comparing Frost competing as a two-way player with the skills of early 1900s Olympian Jim Thorpe.

"He's a brilliant athlete," Walsh said of Frost. "A gifted man. You can't have a great athlete like him on the sideline keeping stats. We call him Thorpe."

Upon hearing that description, Frost tongue-in-cheek asked beat writers if his coach had been drinking. But soon Frost carried two sets of pads and two jerseys to practice, working at two positions.

"It took me by surprise when I first heard it," he said. "It went through my mind that maybe they weren't happy with my quarterbacking. But that was a selfish way to react.

"The physical part, I don't worry about. Football is a game of contact.

Sept. 27, 1994: Scott working at safety during a Stanford practice.

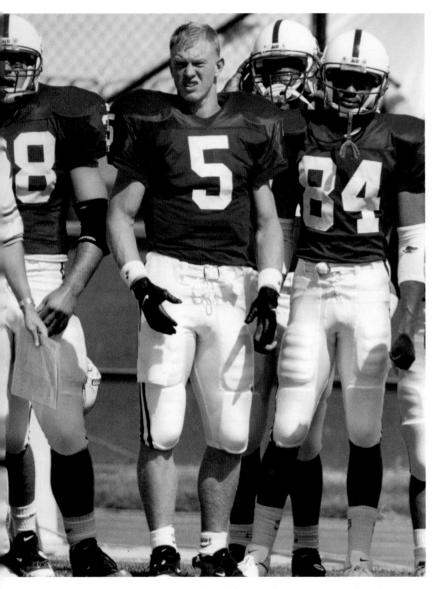

Sept. 27, 1994: Scott on the sidelines at the Arizona game where he starts for Stanford at safety.

There may be a couple of quarterbacks out there who don't feel like that, but in my opinion they shouldn't be on the field."

Frost started five games at free safety in 1994, and played the final 2½ games at quarterback after Stenstrom suffered a broken finger on his throwing hand. Frost rallied Stanford to an upset of No. 12 Washington the day Stenstrom was injured. The Cardinal lost the final two games to Oregon and Cal, finishing 3-7-1.

Frost completed 33 of 77 passes for 464 yards and two touchdowns and rushed 38 times for 193 yards and two touchdowns.

Nine days after the season finale, Walsh resigned amid reports of turmoil on the team. A group of players met with the athletic director to complain about the program's progress, and one of the topics was Frost starting at quarterback late in the season over another backup.

Earlier in the season, after a loss at Arizona in which Frost started at free safety, he questioned the team's enthusiasm and toughness.

"That's OK with me for him to say that," Walsh said. "That shows some leadership and competitiveness. That's great to hear."

With Walsh gone, speculation began immediately about Frost transferring to Nebraska.

It happened, but not until after Frost returned to Stanford's campus for the start of the second semester. Once he got there, he realized his dissatisfaction was too great to continue, and he contacted NU coach Tom Osborne about a home-state return — and thanked Osborne for never pressuring him to transfer, and insisting he give Stanford one more look.

Larry Frost said at the time Scott's move to Nebraska came down to one thing.

"He just didn't like losing," Larry said. "He's a tremendous competitor. He's never lost at anything in his life."

Leave it to Osborne to greet what became one of his biggest recruits with this plain-label assessment: "A guy with his ability would surely fit in somewhere."

LONG BEFORE SCOTT FROST arrived in Lincoln, he impacted Nebraska's quarterback situation.

Even with four scholarship players at that position returning in 1993, Osborne set his sights on Frost, promising the high school All-American that NU would take no other quarterbacks if he would sign.

When Frost committed to Stanford just before signing day, Nebraska tried to get Millard North's Todd Doxzon. But he had already committed to Iowa State.

"That hurt us," Osborne said. "We'd have taken Todd Doxzon in a minute. But sometimes you roll the dice and don't win."

The gamble left Osborne without an incoming scholarship quarterback for the first time in his coaching career. And with Tommie Frazier claiming the starting job in 1992 midway through his freshman season, the depth chart at quarterback grew dicey in 1993 and 1994.

Touted prospect Ben Rutz transferred to a junior college and eventually Kansas. Tony Veland, after suffering multiple injuries, switched to free safety — a path that led him to the NFL and a Super Bowl championship.

For 1994, Osborne had two "top-flight" quarterback prospects, but couldn't get either to say yes as Frazier entered his junior season.

"They made comments about Tommie being here for a couple of more years," Osborne said. "Having Tommie here has been more of a blessing than a curse, but there has been a downside to it with recruiting."

Donovan McNabb was close. Then Charlie McBride's recruiting pitch to the future NFL standout got sabotaged.

"Danny Nee pissed me off so bad," said McBride, NU defensive coordinator.

McNabb wanted to play football and basketball in college. He visited Nebraska, where McBride escorted him to the Devaney

Center to meet the Husker hoops coach. Nee walked right past McNabb; he didn't want a football player on his team.

"(McNabb) would've come here," McBride said. "But he went to Syracuse because they said he could do it."

The lone scholarship quarterback NU landed for 1994 was Jon Elder from Sioux City, Iowa, who left that fall for Wayne State. So Nebraska, because of injuries and departures — including blood clots that knocked out starter Frazier — entered a 1994 game against Wyoming with the following quarterback depth chart:

1. Scholarship junior Brook Berringer.

2. Walk-on sophomore Matt Turman.

3. Walk-on freshman Adam Kucera, who until a month earlier was a student manager.

4. Walk-on freshman Ryan Held, who until three weeks earlier was a split end. (Held now is Nebraska's running backs coach).

Berringer suffered a collapsed lung against Wyoming. It deflated again at halftime the next week against Oklahoma State, so Turman finished and started the next game at Kansas State.

Even though Frazier and Berringer returned to mostly full health by season's end to lead Nebraska to a national championship victory over Miami in the Orange Bowl, the circumstances along the way showed how important it was for Osborne to land an experienced, high-end quarterback who could play in 1996 after those two graduated.

NEBRASKA'S 1994 QUARTERBACKS

TOMMIE FRAZIER

BROOK BERRINGER

MATT TURMAN

Frost's transfer to Nebraska in January 1995 gave him a year and a half to get acclimated before becoming eligible.

Any expectation of a quiet transition ended quickly.

Frost's quick decision to transfer at midyear left him without time to find a winter coat. Seeing him pictured in the Daily Nebraskan his first day on campus wearing Stanford letterman's apparel caused some fans to cringe and teammates to seethe.

Years later, fullback Joel Makovicka acknowledged initial hard feelings toward Frost and his snub of the program out of high school.

"If we're being honest, the guys were pissed," Makovicka said in "Unbeatable," The World-Herald's book about the 1994-97 seasons. "He had a lot to prove to a lot of the guys."

Chilly receptions from some teammates were common. So were the usual locker room high jinks for high-profile newcomers, such as messing with your belongings and taping shut your dressing stall.

But it was during Frost's season quarterbacking the scout team that he ran the gantlet and proved he belonged.

He endured daily duress from the Blackshirts, who thumped him on every option play and sometimes ripped off his helmet and tossed it downfield. Brothers Christian and Jason Peter were particularly ambitious. Frost later noted that he thought Jason hit harder, but Christian punched harder.

In a 1996 in-season episode of Tom Osborne's weekly TV show, there's a panel of Osborne, Frost and host Bill Doleman openly discussing the practice shenanigans. Doleman asked Frost which was more difficult: His year sitting out, or playing under ever-present scrutiny as the successor to Frazier.

As Frost noted the difficulty of both, Osborne interjected with: "You got beat around a little on the scout team."

April 22, 1995: Scott plays in Nebraska's spring game.

Frost: "I got in my share of fights with Christian and Jason Peter."

Osborne: "Yeah, Christian and Jason grabbed him by the throat every night. So this is a little bit easier."

Doleman to Osborne: "You let that happen to your quarterbacks?"

Osborne: "Sometimes. You can't protect them forever. It does toughen them up."

To which Frost, nodding toward Osborne, added with a smile: "They kind of turn their back on the scout team."

Off the field, Frost's plan to keep a low profile during his transfer season didn't work out. During Nebraska's run to the 1995 national title, he got caught in the middle of teammate Lawrence Phillips' dispute with former girlfriend Kate McEwen, a Husker women's basketball player.

McEwen was at Frost's apartment hours after Phillips was the star in a win at Michigan State. Later that night, Phillips learned McEwen was there, scaled the balcony to the third floor and tried to drag McEwen out with Frost trying to stop it.

The incident drew immediate nationwide attention and lingered through the season as Phillips — at first dismissed from the team — was allowed to return after a six-game suspension.

In spring 1996, most of the attention on Frost returned to football as he competed with Turman, Monte Christo and Frankie London for the No. 1 quarterback job.

By the end of spring ball, teammates openly praised Frost for his ability and toughness. And Osborne added this sweetener:

"Scott Frost has all the ingredients to be a great player."

Sept. 11, 1995: Scott at practice. He spent the 1995 season quarterbacking the scout team and proving his mettle.

HUSKER FROST 'APPRECIATES' SUPPORT OF TEAMMATES

BY LEE BARFKNECHT

Nebraska football fans sweating over how good the quarterbacking will be this season can dry off now, Husker defensive tackle Jason Peter said.

Stanford transfer Scott Frost has shown his new teammates enough this spring, Peter said, to maintain hope for a third straight national championship.

"He'll do fine this fall," Peter said. "Just his athletic ability alone makes him a great quarterback. If he gets out of the pocket, he's tough to get hold of. And in the pocket, he's got a rifle arm.

"A lot of people question whether he'll be able to handle it. But he started a couple of games when he was at Stanford and led them to a big win over Washington. He knows what he's doing."

A smile raced across Frost's face upon hearing the comments from Peter.

"I appreciate that from a great player like him," Frost said. "What's important to me about that is even if the fans are just looking for someone who isn't going to screw up, I'll know I have the confidence of my teammates to go perform well. And that's all that matters to me."

Frost entered spring practice second on the depth chart. But the 6-foot-3, 215-pound junior from Wood River, Neb., has moved into the starting spot in the race to replace Heisman Trophy runner-up Tommie Frazier.

Frost and the rest of the Huskers wrap up spring practice today with the Red-White game at 1 p.m. at Memorial Stadium.

In the three previous major spring scrimmages, Frost ran 22 times for 172 yards (a 7.8 average) and one touchdown. He completed 13 of 31 passes (41.9 percent) for 235 yards, two touchdowns and two interceptions.

Frost said statistics aren't important right now.

"I just wanted to perform like I could, and hopefully the rest would take care of itself," he said. "I feel a lot better than I did at the start of spring ball. There was a lot to learn.

"I tried to pick it up quick. Now, it's a matter of keeping everything in my head and finding out a few more fine points about the offense. For the most part, I think I've got it tackled. I can't wait to get going this fall."

Frost's desire to focus on the future shows in his reluctance to talk in depth about two areas of his past.

The first is the two seasons he spent at Stanford, where he started two games at quarterback and five at safety. Frost said he picked the Cardinal over Nebraska out of high school because he thought playing for Bill Walsh — ex-coach of the San Francisco 49ers — could help him get a head start to pro football.

Walsh eventually left Stanford, and so did Frost. His arrival in Lincoln in January 1995 generated big headlines.

"Obviously it wasn't a great experience at Stanford or I wouldn't have transferred back here," Frost said. "I wasn't comfortable out there. That's all I really want to say about it.

"I wanted to come back and give this a shot. I was pretty excited about the opportunity I would get here. It looks like it's all going to turn out for the best."

March 30, 1996: Scott eludes defenders during a spring scrimmage inside Cook Pavilion.

While sitting out as a transfer last season, Frost became part of a front-page story when ex-Husker I-back Lawrence Phillips assaulted Kate McEwen, an NU women's basketball player. McEwen, a former girlfriend of Phillips, was in Frost's third-floor apartment when Phillips scaled a balcony and entered a sliding glass door at 4:44 a.m. last Sept. 10.

Frost did no interviews at the time of the incident, and has said little since.

"I was bombarded at the time, so I didn't talk to anyone," he said. "So many people were looking for the negative side of it. They were trying to accuse people of this and that.

"It boiled down to a situation where a college kid (Phillips) made a mistake. And he paid for it pretty heavily."

Phillips was suspended for six games last season. He also was placed on a one-year probation after pleading no contest to misdemeanor charges of third-degree assault and trespassing.

Frost likened his involvement in the incident to that of an innocent bystander.

..."I got myself into a situation in which I didn't know what was going on," he said. "I did what I could to handle it the best I could. ..."I'm glad Coach Osborne handled it the way he did."

Frost said that after a year out of the football spotlight, he's not sure what the man on the street thinks about him as a player. In last year's Red-White game, Frost threw for a record three touchdowns during mopup time with the third and fourth units.

Does Frost need to establish an identity in today's scrimmage?

"I don't see it that way," he said. "It's unfortunate how labels get tacked on to people. In the past, fans labeled Brook Berringer a passer and Tommie Frazier a runner, but both could do the other thing pretty well, too.

"Hopefully, I won't get a label. I hope people will think I can run and pass."

Frost said he hopes fans do come to think of him as a contributor and not just someone whose main goal is to avoid turnovers.

Scott and Ahman Green pose for the cover of The World-Herald's 1996 college football preview section.

"The idea of not making mistakes isn't an altogether stupid philosophy," Frost said. "At the same time, you need a guy out there who can make plays.

"That's going to come when whoever starts at quarterback — hopefully me — gets through a few games, makes some plays and people start trusting you to do things. Right now, they look at the I-backs like Ahman Green and Damon Benning to make a lot of big plays.

"But the guy at quarterback has got to be able to do quite a bit, too."

SEPTEMBER 7, 1996

GOAL OF THREE-PEAT STOKES HUSKER FIRE

BY LEE BARFKNECHT

In five of the six major spectator sports in America — pro football, pro basketball, pro baseball, pro hockey and college basketball — at least one team has won titles in three consecutive seasons.

The exception is college football. Nine teams were in position to finish No. 1 three straight times since the current polling system began 61 years ago. But all fell short, including Alabama in 1966 despite going 11-0.

Today, Nebraska becomes the 10th back-to-back national champion to try to start a run into sports history when it opens the 1996 season at home with an 11:10 a.m. game against Michigan State (1-0) on ABC-TV.

The magnitude of what the top-ranked Huskers could accomplish isn't lost on the players.

"It's in the back of your head," junior rush end Grant Wistrom said. "It can't help but be there."

During summer workouts at Memorial Stadium, the scoreboard flashed the phrase "Three-Peat."

"When we were in the dog days of those workouts," senior linebacker Ryan Terwilliger said, "somebody would bring it up and it would help us get through."

Tom Osborne, who throughout his 24 years as head coach has preached looking past no one, even acknowledged the big picture.

"We've mentioned it," he said. "We've got an opportunity to do something nobody has done.

"On the other hand, I don't know if that's important right now. Talking about a title or something else that might happen three or four

Or is it?

"Coach Osborne doesn't show it as much as we do," senior rush end Jared Tomich said. "But his fire and desire is just as high as ours to win a third one in a row."

But the time for talk is over. Does Nebraska have the talent and makeup to win a third straight national championship?

Osborne answered yes, but with another qualifier.

"The cupboard's not bare," he said. "But in the minds of many in the public, we're so good that if we play well nobody will beat us. I know that's not true."

Some of that thinking also was present in 1972, when Nebraska was coming off back-to-back national championships.

"I don't remember as much hoopla then as there is going into this season," former NU Assistant Coach John Melton said. "Of course, in Nebraska, people figure you're going to win the national championship every year anyway so there's always some talk about it."

The Huskers open their current run for a third straight title with some similarities to 1972 — a preseason No. 1 ranking, three or four national honors candidates and a highly publicized new quarterback in Stanford transfer Scott Frost of Wood River, Neb.

Frost said he doesn't sense that the 1996 team is preoccupied with history or coincidence.

"A lot of times when people stumble in their attempt to repeat or three-peat, it's because they are focused on last year and living in the past," he said. "Here, I see more effort and

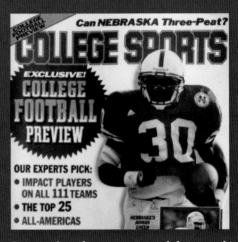

Pressure for a three-peat national championship

sweat on the field this year than I did last year. So I don't think anybody is looking back."

To outsiders, Osborne said, the biggest question mark for Nebraska is whether Frost can take over for All-American Tommie Frazier and Brook Berringer.

"We lost two quarterbacks who proved they could win and had great ability," Osborne said. "But Scott Frost has all the ingredients to be a great player."

Frost, who turned Osborne down out of high school to join Coach Bill Walsh at Stanford, said coming back to his home state to start at quarterback will fulfill a dream.

"Sitting around for the last year and a half since I transferred has been tough on me," Frost said. "But playing Saturday will be a moment I'll

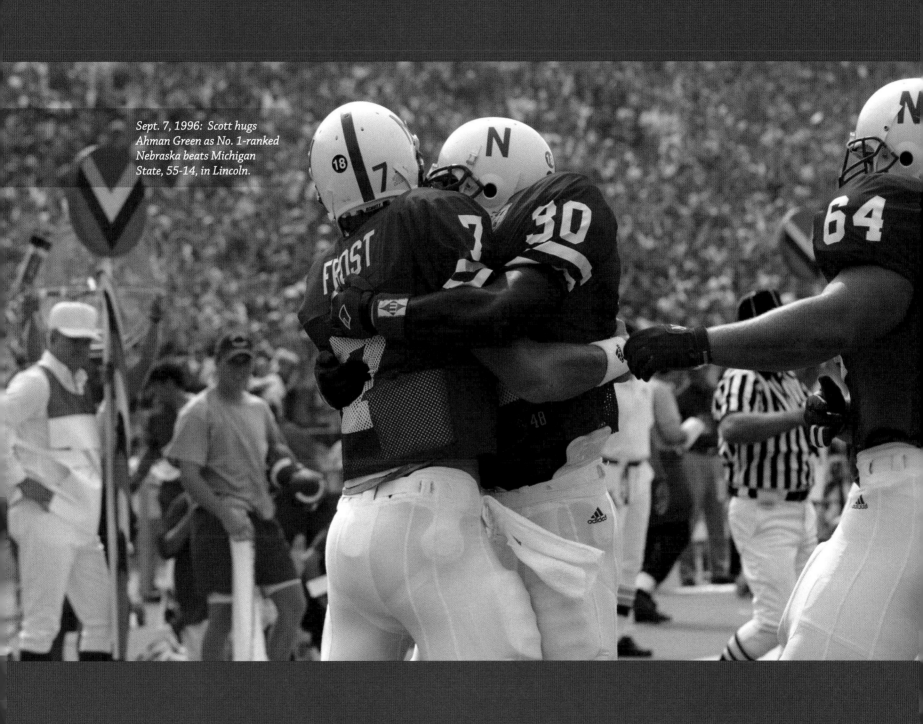

Sept. 7, 1996: Scott hugs Ahman Green as No. 1-ranked Nebraska beats Michigan State, 55-14, in Lincoln.

OCTOBER 17, 1996

NU'S FROST LEARNS TO COPE WITH SPOTLIGHT AT QB

BY LEE BARFKNECHT

Scott Frost came into the quarterback job at Nebraska aware of the attention that goes with it.

He grew up in the state. His parents were athletes at the school. He was recruited by NU, and even though he first attended Stanford, he transferred back to Nebraska to compete for the position.

Sept. 21, 1996: Tom Osborne's support of Scott never wavers despite a 19-0 shutout loss at Arizona State.

But none of that background, Frost said Wednesday, fully prepared him for the hold that being the Huskers' starting quarterback has taken on his life.

"The thing you can't get used to is how continual it is," he said. "Football never goes away.

"It's tough to ever get your focus off of it because everywhere you turn, there is something that has to do with football."

Making the spotlight even brighter and hotter is Frost's role as the successor to Tommie Frazier, who led Nebraska to back-to-back national titles and is generally considered the school's best quarterback ever.

Frost's struggles in his first two starts, which included Nebraska's first loss in 27 games, led to widespread criticism in print and on talk shows.

But the clatter appears to be subsiding as Frost prepares for Saturday's 2:34 p.m. game at Texas Tech.

Nebraska's three-game winning streak, in which it has outscored opponents 153-12, and Frost's improved performance in those games (59.2 percent completions and a hand in four touchdowns) has earned him compliments.

"Scott Frost is playing very well, and we're pleased with his progress," Nebraska coach Tom Osborne said.

"He's becoming the quarterback we knew he was," NU Receivers Coach Ron Brown said.

"He got past the hype," Husker tight end Sheldon Jackson said. "There was a lot of it the first two games, but there's not near the pressure on him now that there was."

Frost said he still hasn't met his own expectations.

"But I think I've come a long way in the last few weeks and earned the respect of my teammates," he said. "Actually, I think I've had it all along, but it probably has increased lately."

Frost said his sense of calm also has increased lately, in part by taking steps to deal with football overload. One way has been to get together with teammates and purposely not talk about football.

"A lot of guys on the team feel the same way that football is always in our face," he said. "So we decided to get together and do other things to take our minds off of it."

Phone calls to his parents two or three times a week, Frost said, are another way to get away from the game if he wants.

"When we talk, they wait for me to bring football up," he said. "If we talk football, it's short and to the point. Then we discuss other things."

Frost also has begun to follow advice that he said was offered by the coaching staff — ignore the intense daily newspaper and television coverage of football in Nebraska.

"You can learn that in a hurry going through a season like this," he said. "You enjoy reading the good things, but the best thing to do is just not read any of it. Usually, the good and the bad get overblown."

Frost said he thought too much was made of some Osborne comments three days after NU's 19-0 loss at Arizona State.

Here was Osborne's response to questions about Frost's ability:

"People can come down on his head all they want. But what else are you going to do? You might as well support the guy. He's the best we've got."

Frost said he wasn't offended by what some interpreted to be a backhanded compliment.

"He got bombarded with questions about me and the team and what went wrong," Frost said. "When you have to answer that many questions, something is going to come out and the media are going to take the most negative thing they can and put that response in the paper even if it wasn't intended to be negative.

"Coach Osborne has supported me. He told me he thought I would be a good player, and if we were going to have a great team that I would be the guy."

Frost said he has stopped worrying about answering his critics.

"Some people want to be critical no matter what," he said. "I could have 12 good games from now to next year, and if I played a bad game next year the critics would show up again."

Frost has found that not everyone in the state has a suggestion on how he can improve.

"I've gotten about 20 letters this season, and every single one has been supportive," he said. "I appreciate the Nebraska fans for doing that.

"The people who step up and say stuff when things go wrong are just waiting to find things to pick on. The true fans are the ones who write you and support you when things are going bad."

EVEN BEFORE NEBRASKA'S 1996 football season began, the Huskers faced an all-out blitz — from the media.

Nearly 100 writers and broadcasters appeared at NU's mid-August media day, including the New York Times, New York Daily News, Chicago Tribune, USA Today, Newsday and Fort Worth Star-Telegram.

One of the two big topics was whether Nebraska could become the first college football program to win three straight championships. It had happened in the other five major spectator sports of the time — the NFL, the NBA, MLB, the NHL and college basketball — but not Division I-A football.

The other subject of high interest was how Frost would replace Frazier, who quarterbacked NU to three straight national championship-deciding bowl games and was voted MVP in each.

"Tommie was a good runner, a good passer and a good leader," Frost said. "When you are strong in more than one area, it makes you a great player. The No. 1 thing is getting the ball in the end zone and winning games.

"Tommie was a master at that. I hope I can do the same."

Nebraska I-back Damon Benning said at the time the difference between Frazier and Frost wasn't as great as outsiders might think.

"They are very similar in demeanor," Benning said. "Neither says a whole lot off the field. But get them on the field and you don't like them because they are doing everything they can to beat you. Scott is a no-nonsense guy."

It didn't take long, though, for critics to find ammunition to attack Frost.

In the 1996 opener, Nebraska's defense and kicking game scored or set up 35 points in the 55-14 romp over Michigan State. And after the 19-0 loss at Arizona State, the Huskers were 97th nationally in total offense.

Osborne, during a series of questions about Frost's play at the next weekly press conference, leaned forward in his chair and raised his voice.

"People can come down on his head all they want," Osborne said as his face reddened. "But what else are you going to do? You might as well support the guy. He's the best we've got.

"Believe me, I know that. I may not know much, but I know that."

FROST REMAINED the starter. Soon, the offense started to click. The Blackshirts continued their high level of play. And poll voters, after just four games, had Nebraska back up to fourth and fifth in the country, which rekindled hope for a national title run.

After a 63-7 rout of Kansas in the season's seventh game, Frost appeared on Osborne's TV show as the star of the game and drew praise from his coach.

Dec. 7, 1996: Scott and Tom Osborne at the Big 12 Championship game in St. Louis. With between 30 and 40 Nebraska players suffering from various stages of the flu, Texas defeats Nebraska 37-27. The loss sent Nebraska to the Orange Bowl where they defeat Virginia Tech.

"You've had a good season and you've played well," Osborne said. "I realize you're under a lot of scrutiny. It's a little like when I followed Bob Devaney. For a while, everybody makes comparisons. But you've been able to block a lot of that out."

Frost replied: "I learned a big lesson the first two weeks about not paying attention to what people are saying. Since then, I just worry about how I'm playing."

Osborne added: "I've been pleased with the way you've handled the pressure. It's not easy when people are talking about you and comparing you."

By the end of the regular season, Nebraska had won the Big 12 North Division and Frost was voted the league's offensive newcomer of the year. A victory over 21-point underdog Texas in the Big 12 championship game would propel NU into the national title chase.

But a seemingly minor decision earlier in the season — Osborne didn't make the Huskers take flu shots — helped derail the title run.

Between 30 and 40 players had the flu during the week or played with it in a 37-27 loss to Texas. The loss sent Nebraska to the Orange Bowl, where it beat Virginia Tech in a half-empty stadium.

The month of preparation out of the national spotlight, however, proved beneficial to Frost. And it gave time for coaches, players, media and fans to reflect on his season.

Frost led NU to an 11-2 record and a No. 6 national ranking. He had a hand in 24 touchdowns and was voted third-team All-Big 12. Frost gave himself a ranking of 6 or 7 on a scale of 10.

"I think I've gotten better as the season has gone on," he said. "I can't wait until next year. The offense pretty much has all of its vital parts back."

FAN REACTION TO SCOTT FROST IN 1996

After Nebraska's shutout loss at Arizona State in 1996, fans were not happy with the Huskers or the new quarterback. A sampling of letters to Voice from the Grandstand in The World-Herald:

- The Blackshirts gave up too many runs early against Arizona State, but settled down. It looks as if they will also have to provide the heart necessary for a winning football team because the offense appears to be a bunch of big egos with no sense of teamwork and no leadership.

- I know it's too much to ask to have another quarterback with the leadership-by-example and high character qualities that Tommie Frazier and Brook Berringer exhibited, but must we now have a quarterback with more arrogance than skill and more talk than action?

  I would suggest he shut up and save the pregame analysis and postgame speeches of why the team failed for people more qualified to speak, the coaches.

- Tom Osborne, let's see what our quarterback of the future, Frankie London, can do.

- With the speed that teams have on defense these days, the option game is becoming a thing of the past. The only way it will still work is with a great option quarterback like Turner Gill or Tommie Frazier. The only trouble is that they only come along every 10 years.

- As the departed Kent Pavelka would have said: Safety, safety, safety.

- Scott Frost is an outstanding athlete playing quarterback, not a great option quarterback. We will still have a good season because of our defense, but don't be surprised if we lose one or two more games.

- Dear Stanford, do you have any more safeties who want to play quarterback at Nebraska?

- Two years ago, one of the best quarterbacks in the history of Big Red football was pulled out of the Orange Bowl because he wasn't moving the ball against Miami.

  Saturday, one of the most overrated quarterbacks in Nebraska history played 55 minutes of chaos.

  Where was Matt Turman? He has been a stable performer for three years. He knows and runs the offense well. Why wasn't he playing after the first quarter of the "Disaster in the Desert?"

  Coach Tom Osborne and Quarterback Coach Turner Gill have a tough decision to make. Over the past three years, the Huskers have groomed three quarterbacks to acquire the knack for the big game. Two of them are no longer with us.

  The good news is that the third still is. Don't let small size and low performance indexes fool you. Sometimes having the eye of the tiger is all you need for a team to rally behind you. Matt Turman might not make All-Big 12, but he knows how to move the yardsticks. The coaches are bringing their prize fighter, Scott Frost, along much too fast. He needs an extra year as an understudy to get the mental part of the game down.

- Remember, Husker fans, Bill Walsh, Super Bowl coach extraordinaire and inventor of the West Coast offense, twice went to tiny Wood River, Neb., to recruit Scott Frost. So did Notre Dame Coach Lou Holtz.

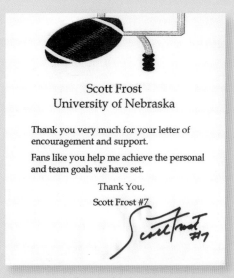

Scott Frost
University of Nebraska

Thank you very much for your letter of encouragement and support.

Fans like you help me achieve the personal and team goals we have set.

Thank You,

Scott Frost #7

Scott occasionally sent thank-you notes to supporters.

- Quarterback Frankie London was hailed as the next Tommie Frazier. Jeff Perino was the next Brook Berringer. They are listed at the middle to bottom of the depth chart. What happened to these two?

  The proper development of the quarterback on a team rests squarely on the quarterback coach. It's his responsibility to bring out the best of all quarterbacks on a team. Seems that while NU was riding high on the talents of Frazier and Berringer, it forgot those two wouldn't be here forever.

- Congratulations to Coach Tom Osborne, his dedicated staff and to all the hard working student-athletes. It has been a great run of games leading up to the two consecutive championships.

  The season is far from over, but I wanted to make sure the fans remember the consistency of the Husker program over the Osborne era. I'm proud to say I respect Osborne and what he stands for. Win or lose, go Huskers.

FROST KNOWS SCORE FOR 1997

BY ERIC OLSON

What Scott Frost knows now that he didn't know then was that as the Nebraska quarterback who followed Tommie Frazier, he was in a no win situation last year.

The Frazier era ended with two national championships, streaks of 36 straight regular-season wins and 25 in a row overall and fan expectations for more of the same. There's no doubt that Frost evolved into arguably the most scrutinized quarterback ever to play for the Big Red. Thing is, Frost really didn't think about it at the time.

"I didn't expect it to be like it was," he said, "but looking back, I'm probably the only quarterback for the last I don't-know-how-long who hadn't played in a game and yet his team was the preseason No. 1.

"It was an unusual situation, and therefore I think I got a little more attention than I deserved — and probably a little more blame than I deserved when we lost early. I definitely used that to my advantage later on in the year. The whole experience helped me grow as a quarterback."

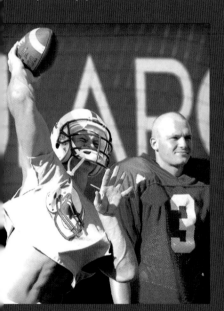

Aug. 9, 1997: Scott, left, warms up as freshman Matt Davison looks on during the first varsity football practice of the fall.

IF ALL YOU LOOKED at from Nebraska's 1997 spring practices were statistics, you never would have guessed Frost was on track to lead NU to a national championship.

In the four major scrimmages, Frost completed 29.8 percent of his passes (14 of 47) for 259 yards, no touchdowns and one interception. It's a good thing quarterbacks coach Turner Gill wasn't a stat head.

"I'm very happy and satisfied with Scott as a passing quarterback," Gill said after that spring. "We want his completion rate over 50 percent. But a lot of things come into play. I look to see if Scott did everything he could to get the ball there."

Aug. 30, 1997: Tom Osborne talks with Scott before the Akron game. On the far left is assistant coach Frank Solich.

Aug. 30, 1997: Tom Osborne leads players onto the field before a game against Akron.

Tom Osborne wasn't a stats-only guy, either.

He knew Nebraska, at times in the spring, had as many as six offensive linemen injured. And that the receiver corps was inexperienced. And that the defense had the potential to rank among the school's best.

Frost's mental work under duress and his physical ability to make something out of nothing was notable. And then there was the intangible of leadership.

Those near the program swore Osborne and Frost could read each other's minds. The comfort level between head coach and quarterback — the two most important figures in any football organization, and not necessarily in that order — spiked in 1997.

That relationship got tested, though, during the season's second game, against the University of Central Florida.

Sept. 13, 1997: Nebraska vs. Central Florida at Memorial Stadium. The boo-birds were out even as Nebraska won, 38-24.

Central Florida, a 42-point underdog, took a 10-7 lead in the second quarter. Osborne, in a planned substitution pattern, brought in Frankie London for a series. London led a touchdown drive.

Frost returned for the next possession, and part of the Memorial Stadium crowd booed him. Most of it came from the student section, but the rumble of discontent was noticeable enough that it became the game's focal point, even after Nebraska rallied to win 38-24.

Osborne scorched the booing fans, saying, "I don't think that has any place in this stadium," before adding that Frost was clearly the No. 1 quarterback.

Frost was hot, too, but at more than the fans. He was ticked at Osborne.

The quarterback, already having taken flak from fans for 18 months, thought his coach had put him in a difficult spot by making it look like he was being benched with NU behind. Osborne later said he felt he had to keep his commitment to London to play.

Frost quickly put his anger at Osborne aside, but not so much for the fans.

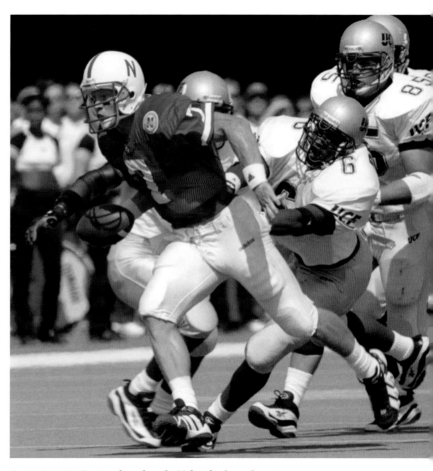

Sept. 13, 1997: Scott endures boos by Nebraska fans after returning to the Central Florida game after backup Frankie London led a touchdown drive. Tom Osborne scorches the booing fans, saying, "I don't think that has any place in the stadium," before adding Frost is clearly the No. 1 quarterback.

In an interview before facing No. 2 Washington the next week, Frost said: "I'll remember my team fondly, but I might not have such special memories of this university."

He turned that emotion into energy, displaying his chops as a championship-level quarterback by leading the No. 7 Huskers

to a 27-14 victory that could have been more lopsided.

The Washington game seemed to unleash an extra level of determination in Frost. Nebraska buried its first five Big 12 opponents by an average score of 47-10 before an early November trip to Missouri (6-3).

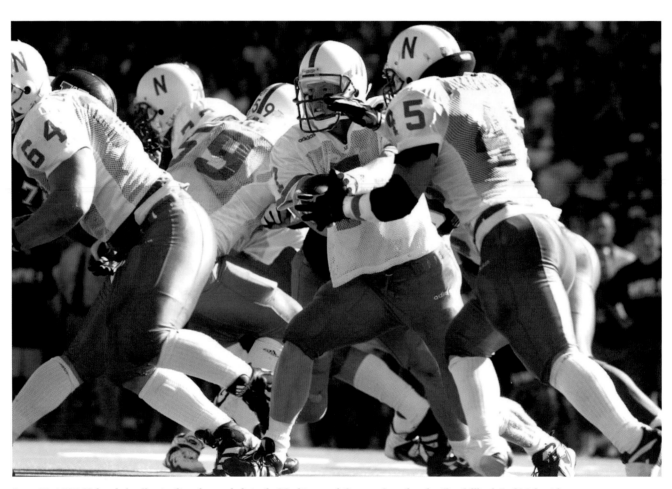

Sept. 20, 1997: Nebraska's offensive line clears a hole in the Washington defense as Scott hands off to fullback Joel Makovicka. No. 7 Nebraska beat No. 2 Washington, 27-14, in Seattle.

Scott walks off the field at Husky Stadium celebrating the Huskers' 27-14 victory, while Washington quarterback Marques Tuiasosopo, No. 11, leaves with his head down.

Nov. 8, 1997: Scott's most famous pass helps keep Nebraska undefeated. The ball ricochets off Shevin Wiggins twice and lands in the hands of Matt Davison. The play sends the game into overtime where Nebraska defeats Missouri, 45-38.

Eric Warfield congratulates Scott after the win.

Tigers quarterback Corby Jones punctured the Blackshirts for 293 total yards and had a hand in four touchdowns as MU led NU 38-31 with 1:02 left in the game.

Frost drove the Huskers 67 yards for a tying touchdown that turned into one of college football's most memorable plays. Frost's 12-yard pass to the end zone deflected off the chest of Shevin Wiggins after a huge hit from behind. As the ball tumbled to the turf, it deflected off Wiggins' foot and Matt Davison plucked it out of the air before it hit the ground.

Then in overtime, Frost ran 12 yards for a touchdown — his fourth of the day — to pull out a 45-38 victory.

"Our dream is to win a national championship," Frost said. "Luckily, we found enough deep down inside to keep those dreams alive."

The only luck needed the rest of the season was after No. 2 Nebraska's 42-17 Orange Bowl romp over Tennessee.

The Associated Press poll appeared a lock to leave Michigan at No. 1 (the final vote count was Michigan 51, Nebraska 14). But the coaches' poll appeared more open to change.

Frost, in the day before the game, grew upset at the thought of finishing 13-0 and not winning a national title. He asked his brother, Steve, to compile talking points for possible use after the game. Frost, who committed those to memory beforehand, spoke during the post-game ceremony on CBS — "I just want to say this about the national championship. If all the pollsters can honestly think after watching the Rose Bowl and watching the Orange Bowl that Michigan can beat Nebraska then go ahead and vote Michigan by all means. I don't think there is anyone with a clear conscious who can say Nebraska and Tom Osborne doesn't deserve a national championship or at least a share of it."

And at the late night press conference, he said to reporters — "I basically have two points for the coaches. One, if you could look in the mirror and say your job depended on playing Michigan or Nebraska, who would you rather play? Two, I can't see how any coach outside the Big Ten or Pac-10 could vote for Michigan . . . It's been split before. It's OK to split it again." The result of the game and the politicking by Frost and other Huskers created change. At 3 a.m., the final coaches' poll showed Nebraska No. 1 with 32 first-place votes to 30 for Michigan.

For that, Osborne said, Frost deserved credit.

"We've had Jerry Tagge," the coach said. "We've had Turner Gill. Had Tommie Frazier. And Scott Frost. Those guys are all in the same category."

Jan. 2, 1998: Scott, above, falls forward after a second-quarter run. Left, Scott stiff arms Tennessee's Deon Grant as he scores his second touchdown of the third quarter. Frost runs for three touchdowns as No. 2 Nebraska defeats No. 3 Tennessee, 42-17, in the Orange Bowl.

PROUD WOOD RIVER BASKS IN SCOTT FROST'S CELEBRITY

BY PAUL HAMMEL

The middle-of-the-night phone call jolted the Rev. Larry Nothstine from a sound sleep Saturday.

"One of my parishioners called at 2:30 in the morning and screamed, 'We're No. 1! We're No. 1!'" said Nothstine, pastor at Wood River United Methodist Church.

Such is the life these days of a minister in the hometown of Scott Frost, the senior quarterback of the national champion Nebraska football team.

Like many small-town homes of Husker heroes, championship fever ran high Sunday in Wood River, a farm town of 1,156 along the Platte River. The news had sunk in: Nebraska had once again been rated the best team in the land.

For many residents, the national title, though shared with Michigan, was a complete vindication for Frost, who had come under fire last year when Nebraska's national-championship drive fell short and who had been booed at a game earlier this season in Lincoln.

Towns like Wood River take extra pride in hometown products who can make the grade with the best athletes in the nation on Nebraska's team.

"You have 80-year-old ladies in town talking about 'our Scott' and 'we hope our Scott can win the game for us,'" said Joe Jack, a high school counselor in Wood River.

That pride might have run even higher this year, when as many as nine of 11 starters on the offensive team hailed from Nebraska, including Frost, fullback Joel Makovicka of Brainard and split end Jeff Lake of Columbus.

While this was Nebraska's fifth national title, it was the first with a starting quarterback from the state.

In Wood River, just about anyone you talk to knows Frost, his parents or his brother, Steve. They have a relative who has played with Scott or for his parents, Larry and Carol, who are both coaches at Wood River Rural High School.

One woman said her son shares a birthday with Scott Frost; another said her family provided sweet corn for the Frost family. "He's one of us," said Nothstine, whose parishioners include the Frosts.

Plans were already being made Sunday to honor Scott Frost with a celebration at the high school, where his jersey has been retired.

A sign reading "Wood River: Home of Scott Frost" was being planned for along U.S. Highway 30.

"All you have to do is tell someone you're from Wood River and the first question they ask is, 'Do you know Scott Frost?'" said Melba Boone, owner of Mel's Country Cafe, a truck stop along Interstate 80.

By Sunday, Frost had already been offered a free meal at the cafe, where a breakfast special — the "No. 7" — had previously been named in his honor. Frost's fame has put Wood River on the map, residents said, and brought recognition to a typical Nebraska farm town.

"We've never had a person with such prominence in sports," said Chick Moyer, a banker. "It's unlikely we ever will again. You hope, but it's very unlikely."

On Sunday, Nothstine began the 10:30 a.m. service with congratulations to Larry and Carol Frost, seated in the back row of the church, and to their son, who was traveling to play in the East-West Shrine Classic game next weekend at Stanford University in Palo Alto, Calif.

After the service, as many people shook hands with the Frosts as with the minister." Football is a religion in this state," Nothstine said. "The mood of the entire state depends on the success of the team. Being from California, I'm not used to that."

Larry and Carol Frost know the feeling. Both grew up in small towns in Nebraska, Larry in Malcolm and Carol in Cedar Rapids. Larry Frost said everyone in town has had some contact with his son.

"They feel kind of responsible for his success, too, and that's neat," he said. "If a kid came out of Los Angeles or Kansas City, only a few people at their school may know him."

At one table in Mel's Cafe, a group from Hastings said they had the same feelings of endearment toward their hometown hero, retiring head coach Tom Osborne.

Michelle Davis said Hastings residents took criticism of the coach a little harder than people in other towns but gloried in his success more.

Her brother, Marc Hultine, said Osborne was like many fathers from small Nebraska towns. "The family comes first with him," Hultine said. "We can relate to him."

In Wood River, celebration of a national championship may last longer and be sweeter than elsewhere across the state or country. "It's going to be a lot of fun around here, for at least a year," Larry Frost said.

Jan. 2, 1997: The Orange Bowl win, and passionate speeches by Scott, help convince coaches to give Nebraska the national championship over Michigan.

SCOTT FROST'S 1996 SEASON

In 1996, Scott Frost hopped into the driver's seat of the nation's most high-powered football program. Nebraska, coming off back-to-back national championships, opened the season No. 1 in the polls. Pressure was high because no college team had won three straight titles.

Frost took over for two of NU's most popular and successful quarterbacks ever: Tommie Frazier and Brook Berringer, as coach Tom Osborne noted before the season. "We lost two quarterbacks who proved they could win and had great ability," Osborne said. "But Scott Frost has all the ingredients to be a great player."

Wingback Jon Vedral said he could sense a change in Frost from competing for the starting quarterback job in the spring to claiming it in the fall. "He's getting that aura of confidence about him I've been looking for. With a quarterback, that's kind of a touchy thing. They're special people who need to know they have that confidence from the coaching staff, knowing that they are 'The Man.' "

Here's how Frost performed game to game:

SEPT. 7, 1996: NEBRASKA 55, MICHIGAN STATE 14
HOME

PASSING:
5-12-0
74 yards
1 TD

RUSHING:
10 for 58 yards
1 TD

In Frost's debut, the offense (298 yards) took a back seat to the defense and special teams, which either scored or directly set up 35 of the 55 points.

SEPT. 21, 1996: ARIZONA STATE 19, NEBRASKA 0
AWAY

PASSING:
6-21-0
66 yards

RUSHING:
10 for
minus-7 yards

The Huskers were shut out for only the third time in Tom Osborne's career. The offense fumbled six times and was nailed three times for safeties as Frost finished with 59 total yards.

SEPT. 28, 1996: NEBRASKA 65, COLORADO STATE 9
HOME

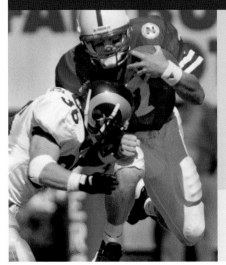

PASSING:
13-18-0
143 yards
2 TDS

RUSHING:
10 for 56 yards
1 TD

Frost had a two-touchdown passing day as Nebraska rolled up 628 yards.

OCT. 5, 1996: NEBRASKA 39, KANSAS STATE 3
AWAY

PASSING:
8-16-1
79 yards
1 TD

RUSHING:
11 for 35 yards

Frost played game manager here as the defense roared and DeAngelo Evans ran for 168 yards.

OCT. 12, 1996: NEBRASKA 49, BAYLOR 0
HOME

PASSING:
8-15-0
178 yards

RUSHING:
12 for 90 yards
1 TD

Frost rolled up 268 yards of total offense while playing just three quarters in a romp.

OCT. 19, 1996: NEBRASKA 24, TEXAS TECH 10
AWAY

PASSING:
4-12-1
55 yards

RUSHING:
14 for 22 yards
1 TD

The offense sputtered, gaining just 238 yards, as Frost ran for less than 2 yards a carry and threw a pick-six.

OCT. 26, 1996: NEBRASKA 63, KANSAS 7
HOME

PASSING:
12-16-0
254 yards
3 TDs

RUSHING:
6 for 35 yards
2 TDs

Frost threw for three touchdowns and ran for two as the Huskers gained 595 yards and built a 42-7 halftime lead.

NOV. 2, 1996: NEBRASKA 73, OKLAHOMA 21
AWAY

PASSING:
10-22-1
163 yards
3 TDs

RUSHING:
8 for 14 yards

Amazingly, NU punted on its first six possessions. Frost threw three touchdown passes after the offense, which gained only 7 yards in the first 20 minutes, got warmed up.

NOV. 9, 1996: NEBRASKA 51, MISSOURI 7
HOME

PASSING:
9-14-0
114 yards
1 TD

RUSHING:
8 for 28 yards
1 TD

The offense contributed 14 points, which was the same as the defense scored and nine fewer than NU's special teams put up.

NOV. 16, 1996: NEBRASKA 49, IOWA STATE 14
AWAY

PASSING:
8-17-0
103 yards
2 TDs

RUSHING:
7 for 28 yards
1 TD

Frost had a hand in three touchdowns on a wet day in Ames, while I-back Ahman Green ran for 214 yards in three quarters.

NOV 29, 1996: NEBRASKA 17, COLORADO 12
HOME

PASSING:
6-14-0
56 yards

RUSHING:
12 for 32 yards

On a rainy, 35-degree day, the offense failed to produce a touchdown. Frost lost a fumble, one of three NU let get away in the second half.

BIG 12 CHAMPIONSHIP
DEC. 7, 1996: TEXAS 37, NEBRASKA 27
ST. LOUIS

PASSING:
15-24-0
155 yards

RUSHING:
18 for 47 yards

National title hopes were crushed as an injury- and illness-plagued NU team lost to the 21-point underdog Longhorns. Frost and the offense played well enough to win, but the defense allowed 503 yards.

ORANGE BOWL
DEC. 31, 1996: NEBRASKA 41, VIRGINIA TECH 21
MIAMI

PASSING:
11-22-0
136 yards

RUSHING:
9 for 62 yards
2 TDs

Frost had one of his more complete games with 198 total yards, and he raced 22 yards for the clinching touchdown.

COLLEGE CAREER STATISTICS

STANFORD 1993
- 11 games
- 2 of 9 passes for 6 yards
- 15 carries for 63 yards
- No TDs

STANFORD 1994
- 11 games
- 33 of 77 passes for 464 yards and 2 TDs
- 38 carries for 193 yards and 2 TDs

NEBRASKA 1995
- Sat out — transfer year

NEBRASKA 1996
- 13 Games
- 104 of 200 passes for 1,440 yards and 13 TDs
- 126 carries for 438 yards and 9 TDs
- Named Big 12 Offensive Newcomer of the Year

NEBRASKA 1997
- 13 Games
- 88 of 159 passes for 1,237 yards and 5 TDs
- 176 carries for 1,095 yards and 19 TDs

COLLEGE CAREER TOTALS
- 48 Games – 26 Starts.
- Record 31-16-1
- 227 of 445 passes for 3,147 yards and 20 TDs
- 355 carries for 1,789 yards and 30 TDs

COLLEGE AWARDS

- Named Big 12 Offensive Newcomer of the Year
- Johnny Unitas Award finalist
- Academic All-American at Nebraska
- First NU quarterback to accumulate more than 1,000 rushing yards and 1,000 passing yards in same season.
- Only native Nebraskan to quarterback the Huskers to a national title.

SCOTT FROST'S 1997 SEASON

In his first season as Nebraska's starting quarterback, Scott Frost led NU to an 11-2 record and was voted the Big 12 offensive newcomer of the year. But some considered that a disappointment because the Huskers were picked in preseason as the nation's No. 1 team.

The spotlight and scrutiny caught Frost off-guard. "I'm probably the only quarterback in I don't know how long who hadn't played in a game and yet his team was preseason No. 1. I think I got a little more attention than I deserved, and probably a little more blame than I deserved when we lost early. The whole experience helped me grow as a quarterback."

After getting booed in a September home game against Central Florida, Frost had a breakout game the next week at No. 2 Washington and went on to lead the Huskers to a share of the national championship with Michigan after a resounding victory over Tennessee in the Orange Bowl.

Here's how Frost performed game to game:

AUG. 30, 1997: NEBRASKA 59, AKRON 14
HOME

PASSING:
7-13-0
67 yards

RUSHING:
11 for 123 yards
2 TDs

Frost scored the first touchdown of the season on a 26-yard run, and the offense scored on nine straight possessions after a missed field goal on the first drive.

SEPT. 13, 1997: NEBRASKA 38, CENTRAL FLORIDA 24
HOME

PASSING:
9-14-0
120 yards

RUSHING:
10 for 52 yards
1 TD

Frost got booed at home when reinserted after backup Frankie London led a go-ahead touchdown drive in the second quarter. An angry Tom Osborne affirmed afterward that Frost was still the No. 1 quarterback.

SEPT. 20, 1997: NEBRASKA 27, WASHINGTON 14
AWAY

PASSING:
8-15-0
88 yards

RUSHING:
29 for 129 yards
2TDs

Frost had his breakout game, leading the upset of No. 2 Washington by rushing for 129 yards and the game's first two touchdowns.

OCT. 4, 1997: NEBRASKA 56, KANSAS STATE 26
HOME

PASSING:
6-13-1
94 yards

RUSHING:
17 for 98 yards
1 TD

"We're as good a team as there is out there," Frost said after leading a third-quarter offensive surge that blew open a tight game.

OCT. 11, 1997: NEBRASKA 49, BAYLOR 21
AWAY

PASSING:
5-8-0
103 yards

RUSHING:
12 for 71 yards
1 TD

The offense ran efficiently as Nebraska pulled away to a 49-7 lead in the third quarter, capped by Frost's 1-yard run.

OCT. 18, 1997: NEBRASKA 29, TEXAS TECH 0
HOME

PASSING:
5-12-1
46 yards
1 TD

RUSHING:
19 for 83 yards

With Frost struggling in the pass game, the offense covered up some inconsistency by grinding out 400 yards rushing.

OCT. 25, 1997: NEBRASKA 35, KANSAS 0
AWAY

PASSING:
4-9-0
33 yards

RUSHING:
21 for 121 yards
2 TDs

On a rainy, 40-degree night, Frost and I-back Ahman Green topped 100 yards rushing each as Nebraska kept the ball on the ground.

NOV. 1, 1997: NEBRASKA 69, OKLAHOMA 7
HOME

PASSING:
6-10-0
107 yards
1 TD

RUSHING:
8 for 66 yards
1 TD

On the day of Osborne's 250th career victory, Frost led the offense to 556 yards and ran for a touchdown.

NOV. 8, 1997: NEBRASKA 45, MISSOURI 38, OT
AWAY

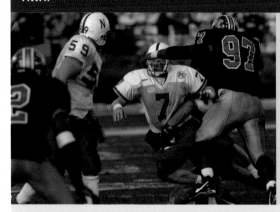

PASSING:
11-24-2
175 yards
1 TD

RUSHING:
23 for 141 yards
4 TDs

Frost ran for four touchdowns and threw for one — completing a deflected pass on the final play of regulation to force overtime — before scoring the winner on a 12-yard run.

NOV. 15, 1997: NEBRASKA 77, IOWA STATE 14
HOME

PASSING:
8-9-0
111 yards
1 TD

RUSHING:
8 for 88 yards
2 TD

Frost was nearly perfect as a passer (8 of 9) as the Huskers bolted to a 63-7 lead at halftime, scoring on their first eight possessions and adding a punt-return touchdown.

NOV 28, 1997: NEBRASKA 27, COLORADO 24
AWAY

PASSING:
7-14-0; 92 yards

RUSHING:
14 for 76 yards; 1 TD

Two late Colorado TDs bothered the Huskers, who were trying to impress pollsters. Said Frost: "Sometimes this whole thing with the polls is bad for you. Early in the fourth quarter, I was trying to hurry up so we could score more points, and that almost cost us the game."

BIG 12 CHAMPIONSHIP
DEC. 6, 1997: NEBRASKA 54, TEXAS A&M 15
SAN ANTONIO

PASSING:
12-18-0
201 yards

RUSHING:
15 for 79 yards
2 TDs

Frost got the offense going early, scoring 37 points in the first half and overall gaining 536 total yards.

ORANGE BOWL
JAN. 2, 1998: NEBRASKA 42, TENNESSEE 17
MIAMI

PASSING:
9-12-0
125 yards

RUSHING:
17 for 60 yards
3 TDs

Frost's play on the field — 185 yards, three touchdowns — and his postgame lobbying for votes in the coaches' poll helped Nebraska split the national championship with Michigan.

MILESTONES AND MEMORIES

Nov. 1, 1997: Scott congratulates Tom Osborne for 250 career victories in 25 years.

Nov. 15, 1997: Tom Osborne's and Scott's last game at Memorial Stadium.

Sept. 29, 2012: Oregon coach Chip Kelly, left, and receivers coach Scott Frost direct the Ducks against Washington State in Pullman.

THE INFLUENCERS

NFL AND EARLY COACHING YEARS: 1998 TO 2015

BY EVAN BLAND

TODD BOWLES DOESN'T NEED to hear the end of the sentence. A book about Scott Frost is coming and ...

"Niiiiice," the head coach of the New York Jets says. "He'll always be one of my favorite people."

Their paths crossed for only a short time. With the Jets in 2000, when Frost enjoyed his best season as an NFL safety and Bowles was his secondary coach. Then again with Cleveland in 2001 when both coincidentally caught on with the Browns.

Bowles didn't consider the youthful quarterback-turned-defender from Nebraska to be a future head coach at the time. But he noticed an unmistakable football intelligence — Frost leaned on it as he switched sides of the ball — as well as an ability to communicate with coaches and teammates, a rare trait for someone in his mid-20s.

Frost credits Bowles for teaching him the proper technique that helped him extend his NFL career a few more seasons. Bowles commends Frost for asking questions and refusing to simply follow orders. Frost wanted to understand the whys, so much so that he had a then-36-year-old Bowles rethinking his own beliefs during some practices.

"I didn't know he was paying that close of attention," Bowles said with a laugh. "I think he's outgrown me and he's probably smarter than I am at this juncture of my life. I'm happy about that. If I could help him with anything, I think that's great. And I know he's done a ton on his own."

The foundation of Frost's résumé of legendary football mentors began in college under Bill Walsh at Stanford and Tom Osborne at Nebraska. But from the moment the Jets took him in the third round (67th overall) of the 1998 NFL draft, Frost continued learning from football masters.

Frost's who's-who list of men he played for and learned from includes Bill Parcells and Bill Belichick of the Jets and Jon Gruden, Mike Tomlin and Monte Kiffin at Tampa Bay. He spent another decade in the coaching ranks under college football movers such as Raheem Morris and James Franklin at Kansas State and Chip Kelly and Mark Helfrich at Oregon.

Picking up a tip here, like how a strong and consistent message from Parcells and Belichick could galvanize an organization. Noting an observation there, like how Tomlin — then the defensive backs coach with the Bucs — treated his players "like men" and inspired them to work toward the same goal.

And that's to say nothing of his time at Oregon, where he acquired firsthand knowledge of Kelly's up-tempo, spread-based attack and later called plays for college football's most prolific offense.

"I've been around a lot of great coaches, and I would have been a fool not to have absorbed a lot from them," Frost said in 2007. "The No. 1 thing I've learned is that to be successful in this business, it has to be about more than wins or losses. If that's all you're worried about, inevitably you are setting yourself up for disaster.

"But if you take a selfless attitude and you're willing to help your players on and off the field, you're going to have something to lean on in the tough times."

Tough times were coming for Frost as he left the Huskers and the glow faded after he quarterbacked the team to a 1997 national title, but so were some invaluable lessons — and he was ready to soak them all in.

July 16, 1998: Scott works out with the Huskers in Lincoln. He said the Nebraska heat and humidity were a lot different than the weather in New York state, where he was headed to play for the New York Jets.

NO NFL TEAM VIEWED FROST as a quarterback prospect. But Dick Haley saw enough to put his reputation on the line for the one-time option operator.

Haley, the director of player personnel for the Jets, persuaded Parcells to select Frost relatively early in that 1998 draft. After all, Frost had posted one of the highest IQ scores at the NFL scouting combine. And his physical measurables — a 4.6 40-yard dash to go with his 6-foot-3, 219-pound frame — were more than adequate for a safety working under Belichick, the defensive coordinator.

"Just do this and make it work," Haley told Parcells. "Don't look back."

The move raised eyebrows in New York. This was a high draft price for a guy whose entire experience on defense was playing linebacker and defensive back at tiny Wood River High in Nebraska and safety for five games at Stanford. Could he really learn a new position and contribute at the highest level?

"(It) is a little bit of a gamble," Parcells said following the draft. "People in the league I respect have told me, 'I don't think you can make this work.'"

The Hall of Famer who began his coaching career at Hastings College in Nebraska joked to Frost that if they couldn't figure things out, they would both be back in Hastings soon enough.

In a more serious assessment, Parcells added: "He's an impressive young man. I like guys who get their teams to the national championship."

Belichick said any drama in the adjustment process was eased by Frost's detailed knowledge of football concepts. Players like him — the current New England Patriots coach noted traits like toughness, work ethic, intelligence and evident communication and leadership skills — aren't as common as coaches would like.

"Scott was very willing to work and learn while I coached him," Belichick said in an interview for this book. "The safety position is the defensive equivalent of the quarterback on offense.

The position involves a lot of decision-making and communication as well as seeing the game from the middle of the field. I hope I was able to teach him the assignments and techniques of his position, which I tried to do to the best of my ability."

Frost had no qualms moving to defense, though he held out hope that maybe the Jets would use him as a change-of-pace quarterback on occasion. Certainly, he insisted then, his ego had no problem with the transition.

"I got all the glamour I needed at Nebraska, and now I'm ready to play football," he said. "I'm in New York City. It doesn't get more glamorous than that."

So Frost traded in No. 7 for No. 47 and became "the chaser instead of the chasee." There were some experiences he could draw on, like his knowledge of Walsh's West Coast offense that was taking over the league. But his defensive skills had atrophied over the years, which became painfully clear as NFL receivers consistently beat him in one-on-one coverage during practice.

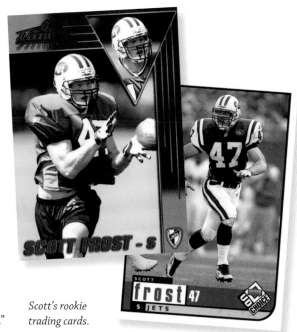

"I know the kid can keep up mentally," Parcells said as the 1998 season opener crept closer. "It's just adjusting to technique. And he's going to be doing it over and over and over again. If he makes it, the upside could be tremendous."

Scott's rookie trading cards.

Aug. 20, 1998: Scott stretches with New York Jets teammates before a preseason game against the New York Giants in East Rutherford, New Jersey.

NEWLY-SIGNED FROST ADJUSTING TO NFL ATMOSPHERE

BY COLLEEN KENNEY

During a mini-camp a few weeks back, Scott Frost called New York Jets wide receiver Keyshawn Johnson crazy.

That's because he thought Johnson, the former No. 1 draft pick out of USC who wrote the book "Just Give Me the Damn Ball," was disrespectful toward Nebraska.

"Keyshawn Johnson seems to be a really nice guy," said Frost, the Nebraska quarterback who led the Huskers to a national title last season. "But he's not afraid to tell you how good he is. The one thing he said that kind of shocked me was, 'Nebraska was lucky they didn't have to play USC in 1995.' "

In 1995, Frost said, Nebraska had one of the best teams in college football history.

"I just kind of laughed," he said, "and I told him I thought he was crazy."

Frost signed a three-year, $1.1 million contract with the Jets on Tuesday night and started training camp Wednesday.

Now Frost has been working out alongside NFL stars he used to watch and admire on TV — Johnson, quarterback Vinny Testaverde, and running back Curtis Martin.

"Your attitude toward those guys," he said, "has to change real fast."

Frost, who will play safety, said the atmosphere during two mini-camps he's attended was "totally different" from his workouts at Nebraska.

"Anytime you join a new team," he said, "you have to get used to the players. But in the NFL it's really different because you have guys from everywhere who are used to being the best people in their

colleges. And none of the people coming in can hold a candle to the rest who have been there for three or four years to begin with.

"So there's a real learning process that takes place."

All the players in the Jets camps seem very confident, he said, even though many of them — and about half of the rookies — won't make it.

"It's everybody for themselves and only the strong survive," he said. "All the clichés that you can think of take place in the NFL. If you can't do the job, they're not going to be loyal to you at all, and you're going to be gone.

"If you don't believe in yourself," he said, "you're going to be the first one gone."

Frost is renting a four-bedroom house on Long Island with three other rookies. Hopefully, he joked, they won't all get cut.

Frost is confident he can successfully make the transition from college quarterback to NFL safety. He doesn't think he'll play quarterback.

At least he hopes not.

"I really don't want to," he said, "because they want me to be a safety, and they think I can be a good safety. If I end up playing quarterback in my first couple years, that probably means it didn't work out at safety and so they're trying me somewhere else."

Frost said that he likes Jets Coach Bill Parcells and that Parcells seems to like him. Parcells, Frost said, likes people who work hard and follow directions — things Frost said his years at Nebraska taught him.

"I really feel confident that playing safety will work out," he said, "and that I'll have as long of a career as God will let me have. But if that isn't the case, there are a hundred other things I could be doing."

Aug. 4, 2000: Scott tackles Green Bay running back Ahman Green during the first quarter of a preseason game. The two Nebraskans were teammates with the Huskers.

ALL THOSE OPTION TECHNIQUES Frost spent countless hours on at Nebraska? Turns out they were "pretty useless" in the NFL.

While everyone else was competing for a job, Frost was still trying to learn a new position. Things didn't come naturally at strong safety, where he was tasked with covering tight ends and being involved in run support. By the end of the season, Frost had appeared in 13 games — mostly on special teams, occasionally in dime packages — and made six tackles along with two pass breakups.

"I didn't have a real good idea of what I was doing," Frost said the next year. "... You can know football as well as you want from the other (offensive) side of the ball, but until you get over on defense and adjusting to that, you're not going to feel real comfortable. It just took me a while."

Progress wasn't evident in 1999, when Frost registered no tackles in 14 games. But a coaching change in 2000 resonated with him as Al Groh replaced a retiring Parcells. With new defensive backs coach Bowles transforming his technique, Frost registered 41 tackles (one sack) and an interception in 16 games, including his first and only NFL start against the Buffalo Bills. He also laid a hit on Bears running back James Allen that forced a fumble in a 17-10 Jets win.

"Obviously it was a little different, but Scott was one of the smartest people as far as learning football and being an astute student of the game that I've probably ever coached from an intelligence standpoint," Bowles said. "To go from offense to defense is not an easy thing, especially as a quarterback. He was tough; he'd stick his face in there and was a very good athlete."

When Groh left to become the head coach at Virginia, Frost worked under new Jets coach Herm Edwards for most of the offseason. The defensive back heard about a series of other front-office shakeups from ESPN2.

On Aug. 27, 2001, Frost was the one changing teams as New York cut him after three seasons. A rib injury from an offseason auto accident had sidelined him most of camp, and depth at his position didn't help.

Cleveland claimed him off waivers a day later, and Frost responded by amassing 16 special-teams tackles in 12 games. But his time with the Browns was short-lived — they later released him, officially, because coaches believed he couldn't fill their need at safety.

Unofficially, speculation in town was he was blamed for a punt-return touchdown the team allowed against New England. Coach Butch Davis promised changes on special teams after that game, and Frost was cut the next day.

Scott participates in a Green Bay Packers tradition — riding kids' bikes to practice throughout training camp.

Most of the rest of Frost's NFL career was behind the scenes. He finished the 2001 campaign with Green Bay but didn't play. A dislocated shoulder in training camp ended his 2002 season with the Packers before it began, and he got to know the franchise's linebackers coach, Bo Pelini.

Frost was dropped by the Packers the following year and signed with the San Francisco 49ers before they became the fourth NFL team to let him go. He finished 2003 with the Tampa Bay Buccaneers — notching a single tackle in four games — before getting cut in the 2004 training camp.

That brief time in Florida stuck with Frost. He picked up the "Tampa 2" defense — a scheme taught by Nebraska native and former Husker player and coach Monte Kiffin that is known for two high safeties and an active middle linebacker — and came to believe it was the toughest for an offense to succeed against. He worked under assistants Mike Tomlin and Raheem Morris, both of whom encouraged him to get into coaching.

SCOTT FROST'S NFL CAREER: 1998-2003

1998-2000: New York Jets
Selected in the third round (67th overall) of the NFL Draft. He plays in 43 games, finishing with 35 tackles, one interception and one sack.

2001: Cleveland Browns
Appears in 12 games, primarily on special teams.
He makes 16 tackles. Season is marred by injuries.

2001-2002: Green Bay Packers
The Packers sign Frost at the end of the 2001 season. During 2002 training camp, he sustains a season-ending shoulder injury.

2003: San Francisco 49ers
Attends training camp but fails to make the team.

2003: Tampa Bay Buccaneers
Signs with the Bucs in December to play special teams and provide depth. Finishes the season playing four games and making one tackle.

"He was really unguarded about his past experiences and didn't lean on it as a crutch," said Tomlin, now head coach of the Pittsburgh Steelers. "I just thought he had the can-do attitude that would serve a guy well in coaching. He was a really good communicator. He communicated well with coaches, he communicated well with fellow players. I also thought that was a skill that would serve him well."

Tomlin continued: "... He is trying to build an environment where the players can be at their best and chase their dreams. It is our job as leaders to provide that. It is less about specific lessons, it is probably more about that. I think that is what I see when I watch his teams play. I see coaches that are doing their thing. I see players that are playing with great energy and doing their thing. I think that is environmental. I know how much he evaluates an environment — an environment that people can excel in. That is what I would hope that he took from the experience."

Dec 2, 2001: Scott plays one season for the Cleveland Browns, appearing in 12 games and making 16 tackles.

HIS TIME IN THE NFL OVER, Frost pondered playing quarterback in Canada. Then he spent about 18 months in Lincoln as a "separation period" from his playing days. Finally, he took a business job in Omaha.

That lasted eight days.

The first in a series of coaching breaks for Frost came when Morris called his former player to tell him he would be defensive coordinator at Kansas State for the 2006 season. The conversation wasn't supposed to be a job discussion, but

Scott was a Kansas State defensive graduate assistant in 2006, during a 7-6 season. The toughest part, he said, was losing 21-3 to Nebraska.

it eventually led to the Nebraska native wearing purple on the sidelines of Bill Snyder Family Stadium as a graduate assistant.

The "G.A." tag was misleading, with Frost serving as the de facto secondary coach on a Ron Prince-led staff that assigned only three full-time assistants to defense. No one knew Morris' defense better than Frost, who helped the Wildcats finish 7-6. The toughest part was losing 21-3 to a familiar team in red when the Huskers trekked to Manhattan in mid-October.

"It was weird," Frost said following that season. "Seeing people I knew and the uniforms I'm used to, it was really weird. In this profession, you'd like to think you can coach exactly where you want. But anybody who has been in it knows you've got to go where the opportunities are.

"I don't have any idea where the good Lord or coaching will take me. But my goal is to stay in it, move up and try to give back."

Frost's upward path took him to Cedar Falls, Iowa, where Northern Iowa coach Mark Farley knew who he was from his Nebraska playing days. But that didn't help much with no full-time coaching experience to put on a résumé and going against nearly 200 other applicants all hoping they could coach linebackers.

Partly on the strength of an endorsement from an equipment manager he had worked with at Kansas in the 1990s and partly on a gut feeling, Farley brought the young 30-something in for an interview.

"I mean, he was a quarterback, he was a defensive back," Farley said. "So I was trying to figure out if he could teach and coach linebackers. That was really my only concern. But when I spoke to him, I could see he had a way to communicate. I would call him a grass coach. You get on the grass, he can show you how to do it as much as tell you how to do it."

Frost accepted the job and began building friendships with staff, including then-tight ends coach Erik Chinander, now Nebraska's defensive coordinator, and quarterbacks coach Mario Verduzco, who now has the same position at NU.

On the field, he made sure linebackers were prepared through film study and tough practices. UNI went 12-1 in 2007, then 12-3 the next year as Frost added co-defensive coordinator duties.

But it was the other stuff that stood out to Farley and many players. The pheasant hunting Frost did with his dog. The pride he made obvious — both vocally and visibly — in his alma mater at Nebraska.

Northern Iowa's Fellowship of Christian Athletes chapter was started by Frost. He started it first among some of his linebackers before eventually opening it up to the entire campus.

"Scott's the whole package," Farley said. "The thing I remember most about him is his relationship with his players is tremendous. He was always a great teacher, but the thing that stood out ... he always had a very calm way of relating to the players and always had good relationships, particularly with the segment he coached for us."

The offseason that followed changed Frost's life forever. Frost met with Oregon head coach Mike Bellotti and his coach in waiting, Chip Kelly, during the national coaches' convention in Nashville, Tennessee. They were interviewing the final dozen or so candidates to become the program's receivers coach and help run an offense that was about to take college football by storm.

As it turned out, the man who landed the open position was a young, unrecommended FCS assistant who wanted to discuss defense for the majority of the meeting.

"We spent 25 minutes talking about tackling," Bellotti said. "And I loved it, actually."

The Ducks had made an offseason commitment to shift to a spread-offense attack with shotgun formations and zone-read concepts. They would need their wideouts to block more and be physically tougher. So it resonated with the 14-year Oregon head coach when Frost passionately broke down tackling techniques. It stuck when he spoke passionately about how the "Tampa 2" defense could stop any attack.

"This is a guy that played quarterback in college and I don't know how much tackling he actually ever did," Bellotti said. "But he talked his way through both the execution of a tackle, how you teach preparation, etc. He wasn't a slam dunk for the job, but he did impress me during the interview and that's why you interview people, just to find out what you don't know about them. Or maybe what you do."

Frost got the job and, in that moment, changed the arc of his career that took off like an Oregon no-huddle drive.

"The No. 1 thing we talked about is bringing an energy to it, bringing a toughness to your players, and also coaching players with the attitude that you care for them," a 34-year-old Frost said at the time. "One of my old coaches talked about (how) players are easy to motivate when you know how to care for them."

Perhaps the most lasting image of Frost in 2009 was what he did after a game. It was national news when Oregon's LeGarrette Blount sucker-punched an opposing playing following an upset loss at Boise State. As Blount left the field, Frost stepped in to restrain the 6-foot-2, 250-pound running back from attacking a heckling fan and prevented further escalation of a dangerous situation.

Meanwhile, Oregon was taking off. It boasted the nation's top scoring offense in 2010, averaging 47 points per outing as the Ducks took an unbeaten record into the national title game before falling 22-19 to Auburn. Twelve-win seasons the following two years put the flashy program into the Rose Bowl and Fiesta Bowl, respectively, before Kelly left to coach the Philadelphia Eagles.

"I couldn't have landed in a better place to learn an offense than at Oregon," Frost said in 2011. "I think (Kelly) does it as well as anybody in the country. ... I'm having fun with what I'm doing right now. I'm anxious to continue to see where it takes me. I think I'd like to become a head coach someday, but I'm definitely not in a big hurry to do that."

New Oregon head coach Mark Helfrich quickly promoted Frost to coordinator for the 2013 season and — in one final career bump that would make him an annual candidate for jobs around the country — handed him play-calling duties and the keys to college football's Lamborghini of an offense.

Most of what he would use, Frost said at the time, came from Kelly.

"He's a sharp guy who gets the big picture," Helfrich said of Frost. "He does a great job identifying with a bunch of guys, which comes in handy when you're dealing with a bunch of different units offensively. Everything meshes well. He's a guy that played. He has that credibility."

The Ducks missed nary a beat, finishing 11-2 that fall and rolling up 45.5 points per game (third nationally). That number

Dec. 30, 2014: Scott, as Oregon's offensive coordinator, talks to reporters during a news conference in Los Angeles. Oregon qualified for the first College Football Playoff and trounced Florida State 59-20 in the Rose Bowl semifinal.

remained nearly identical in 2014 as Oregon qualified for the first College Football Playoff and trounced Florida State 59-20 in the Rose Bowl semifinal. Oregon lost to Ohio State 42-20 in the national championship game. Frost was a finalist for the Broyles Award, given to the country's top assistant.

Meanwhile, quarterback Marcus Mariota won the Heisman Trophy under Frost's tutelage and parlayed it into the second pick of the 2015 NFL draft. With Frost calling the shots, he threw for 3,783 yards and 38 touchdowns (with just two interceptions) while also rushing for 669 yards and 14 scores. His 53 total touchdowns — he also caught a TD pass — tied for the most in Heisman history.

Mariota was a Frost fan.

"He's a stern leader," Mariota told The Oregonian that season. "He wants what's best for his players. And he's very smart. He knows how to handle different game situations. Just one of those guys you want to play for. The type of relationship I have with Coach Frost, he has with every single player on the team, and that's pretty special."

In all, Oregon went 79-15 (.840) during Frost's seven-year run in Eugene. The scoring offense never dipped below fifth nationally in the last six seasons as the high-flying unit — one that strived to snap the ball 10 seconds after the previous play ended — carried the Ducks to a pair of title games and produced NFL players annually.

The job offers piled up along with the points. Frost interviewed at Boise State and was involved with Colorado State in 2014 before removing himself from consideration. The rising offensive coordinator was also linked to the opening at Tulsa that same year.

Not until Central Florida came calling following the 2015 season did Frost finally become a head coach. The recruiting area was ripe with fast athletes who could run his up-tempo offense. Now was his chance to put to use a lifetime of gridiron guidance.

Sept. 13, 2014: Oregon quarterback Marcus Mariota jokes with Scott before a game against Wyoming. Mariota won the Heisman under Scott's tutelage. "The type of relationship I have with Coach Frost, he has with every single player on the team, and that's pretty special," Mariota said.

CENTRAL FLORIDA IS PERFECT IN FROST'S CLIMB TO MAJORS

BY TOM SHATEL

Head coach Scott Frost.

He looked the part the other day at the University of Central Florida. He sounded the part, saying, "Fans better buckle their seat belts because we're going to punch the accelerator and go fast around here, and sooner or later that's going to lead to a lot of success."

It's the role of a lifetime for a small-town Nebraska kid who grew up with mom and dad, Carol and Larry, coaching him in football and life.

His résumé looks like a Hall of Fame ballot. Tom Osborne. Bill Walsh. Bill Parcells. Bill Belichick. Jon Gruden. Chip Kelly. Frost played or coached for that Who's Who list.

It's all there, pointing to this time and this place. Wait. Central Florida?

Especially that part.

Frost has treated his coaching career like a chessboard, and this might be the most important move of all.

Central Florida is a school with 60,000 students. It's in Orlando, surrounded by golf courses and talented high school football players.

The Knights play in the American Athletic Conference. They don't have major conference expectations but have access to major games. Two years ago, Central Florida beat Baylor in the Fiesta Bowl.

So this is where a young coach can make a name for himself — and figure out who he is — without getting swallowed whole. How many young coaches took the wrong first job and were never heard from again?

Frost, it seems, is a college football history major.

"I've talked to Scott for 10 years about being a head football coach," said Matt Davison, Frost's good friend and former Husker teammate.

"Scott has never been motivated by the big paycheck. He hopes to be coaching for the next 20 years, not get a big paycheck and coach for the next three years.

"That's why he talked a lot about certain jobs across the country where you can really do well. There are some where you take it and a few years later you ask yourself, 'Why did I take this job?' Scott didn't want that. He talked about certain places and targeted those jobs, kept up with them. Central Florida is one of those places."

It looks like a better starter job than, say, Purdue, Kansas or ... Nebraska?

Tom Osborne moved from Bob Devaney's offensive coordinator to head coach at NU in 1973. That worked out OK.

But even Osborne would tell you there were rough spots, alumni who were after his job in his fourth year, and he got room to grow in a high-pressure job from having a boss (Devaney) who believed in him.

Frank Solich and Bo Pelini were not as fortunate. Their first jobs were in an environment that demands championship results against crowded dance floors in the Big 12 and Big Ten.

How would history be different if Solich and Pelini had started their careers at Ohio University and Youngstown State?

Urban Meyer and Nick Saban cut their teeth in the Mid-American Conference. Jim Harbaugh's first gig was at the University of San Diego. Then there are Bob Stoops and David Shaw, who won big after getting the Oklahoma and Stanford jobs as coordinators.

History shows that successful coaches usually started small. As Nebraskans prepare to follow their native son, the expectation is that Frost will fall into that category.

"Scott is very bright. Good values. I expect he'll do a good job," Osborne said Friday while taking a break from his duty on the College Football Playoff committee.

"One of the leagues I follow (on the committee) is the American Athletic Conference. It's pretty competitive. A pretty fast league. They play good football. I think Scott will be able to get a lot of players down there to do well in the league. They don't have the high expectations other leagues do. It's a good situation. There's a lot of upside."

Frost's chessboard had a couple of intriguing moves early. The former Nebraska option quarterback played safety in the NFL. After his career ended, he worked as a defensive graduate assistant at Kansas State for Raheem Morris, one of his coaches at Tampa Bay. Then he took a job as linebackers coach and later co-defensive coordinator at Northern Iowa.

"These are not moves that most championship quarterbacks make," Davison said. "They're looking to get higher-profile jobs, coordinator jobs. Scott wanted to get experience coaching defense. He knew it would make him a better head coach. He always had a plan."

Dec. 2, 2015: Central Florida President John C. Hitt, left, and Athletic Director Danny White, flank Scott, the new Central Florida coach, during a news conference in Orlando.

But the reason Frost was such a hot coaching commodity — turning down offers last year — was his role in the Oregon offensive machine. Offense is the rage in college football. Chip Kelly's scheme is like "Star Wars," and athletic directors are lined up like fans in Darth Vader gear.

The time may have been right. Oregon took a step back this year. Kelly's offense is mocked in the NFL. But the up-tempo, fast-break stuff is all over college football. With all the speed on Florida high school fields, the Frost-Central Florida marriage looks perfect.

But aren't we the least bit curious to see if an old Osborne/Nebraska kid will incorporate some old-school power stuff, too, now that he's in charge? You bet we are.

"I expect Scott to use tempo, going with what he did at Oregon and with all the speed he can get down there," Davison said. "But I expect him to try and build an offensive line that is able to run some of the power stuff we had at Nebraska. If he can find the players to do both, that will be a lethal offense."

What about Frost's staff? Frost has been around long enough to have plenty of contacts. He has already hired Colorado receivers coach Troy Walters and Ryan Held, head coach at Northeastern Oklahoma A&M who was a player and undergraduate assistant at Nebraska in the 1990s.

Davison predicts Frost's staff will be full of youth and energy and good recruiters, but says he won't be afraid to bring in veteran assistants who aren't "yes" men.

There's not a long list of former Huskers who became head coaches. Will Frost be the most successful? Finally, it's time to start watching.

"When Scott played, I never really knew if he wanted to be a coach, but he had all the attributes you'd want," Osborne said. "He was a great leader. And he did not always have a smooth career. The fans gave him a hard time at times, but he stuck in there, never complained and became a very good quarterback and leader.

"You know, today you see quarterbacks go to the line of scrimmage and look over to the sidelines and wait for the call. When Scott played, 60 or 70 percent of the time we were checking (into another play). The quarterback did that. He was a confident guy. Very smart guy."

How smart?

"His brother has won on 'Jeopardy!'," Davison said. "And Scott watches 'Jeopardy!' all the time. He's always watching the game show channel. He loves golf, too. His dog is named 'Bogey,' and now he's living in Orlando and he's got a lot more money for me to take off him on the golf course."

He'd probably be good at chess, too.

FROST MAY HAVE LEFT Nebraska, but Nebraska never left him.

A 20-year sojourn encompassing an NFL career and rise through the coaching ranks often felt tinged with the inevitability that the native son would one day wind up back home.

Frost was on the Memorial Stadium sidelines during his rookie season in 1998, taking advantage of a Jets bye week to watch the Huskers trounce Washington 55-7. He was present in 2001 when "Black 41 Flash Reverse" entered NU lore and the third-ranked Big Red toppled No. 2 Oklahoma 20-10.

When Frank Solich fired three defensive coaches in 2002 following Nebraska's worst regular season in 41 years, Frost — then on injured reserve with the Packers — agreed to help through the Independence Bowl as a grad assistant.

"Scott is planning on doing this for the bowl game and will resume his pro career," NU defensive line coach Jeff Jamrog said while filling in for Solich on his weekly radio show. "This is a short-term deal, but in our situation we are very excited."

Frost popped back home for the Cornhusker State Games on multiple occasions. Sometimes he was part of a basketball team — "I do everything but shoot. I play good defense and I'm going to stick to that." — and other times he completed in field events. He swept gold medals in the long jump (20 feet, 10 inches) and shot put (48 feet, 4 inches) in the men's 30-34 category in 2006.

There was 2003, when Frost and fellow ex-Husker Cory Schlesinger worked a Nebraska summer camp as instructors. In 2004 he was one in a line of guests on a short-lived television show featuring former NU football players hunting and fishing in the state. He was a co-owner along with the likes of teammate Aaron Taylor and Dan Whitney (Larry the Cable Guy) of the Scarlet and Cream Letter Club sports bar — a restaurant packed with Husker memorabilia — that opened in 2006 near Village Pointe in Omaha.

All the while, Frost bled Husker red. Never was it more evident than 2005 when, after witnessing a 40-15 Nebraska loss at

July 18, 1999: Scott competes in the shot put during the men's open competition at the Cornhusker State games. His mom, Carol, competes in the shot put and discus.

Kansas from the stands, he wrote a 2,600-word blog post chronicling the downfall of his beloved program.

"Sometimes I think I care too much ..." began the piece, which some call the "Manifrosto." Among the thoughts was a prediction: "I want to become a college football coach, and I plan on looking for a place to start a career in that field after this season is over."

Nebraska media sought out Frost for comment in December 2002 when rumors circulated that Green Bay assistant Bo Pelini would be joining the Huskers staff. He was back in the news in 2011, when his father, Larry, said his son would "love to be on the staff" at Nebraska. It ultimately didn't work out, as Pelini promoted NU assistant Tim Beck to the offensive coordinator position.

June 21, 2002: Scott helps out at a summer football camp at Nebraska's Memorial Stadium.

FIRST DOWNS AND SECOND GUESSES

BY TOM SHATEL

Perhaps a Frost-NU reunion can be later.

Get me rewrite on that fairy tale. According to two sources close to the situation, Scott Frost is not coming back to Nebraska to take the job that, you know, is not open yet.

Some immediate thoughts:

1. There's no controversy here. Frost is not being shunned by Nebraska nor is he turning his back on his alma mater. Frost wanted to call the plays — for the job that's not open yet — and Bo Pelini was never going to agree to that. Neither man is wrong. There's no bad guy.

Frost will always be a Nebraska boy and Husker legend, but his ultimate loyalty must be to himself and his career. If he thinks two years of learning under pinball wizard Chip Kelly qualifies him to become an offensive coordinator who calls the shots, more power to him. If he wants to stay and develop more under Kelly, that's great.

I have not talked to Frost. But his former NU teammates say he wants badly to coach at Nebraska again. He also apparently wants to do it his way. There's nothing wrong with that. If he considers similar jobs at Oregon and Nebraska a lateral move, that says something, too. It says the former Husker is being loyal to himself.

2. If Pelini is hiring a replacement for Shawn Watson — more on that later — then the head coach needs to hire someone he trusts and is entirely comfortable with. It's a big hire. Pelini knows Frost, but not that well. He likes him. He'd like Frost to join the staff, but not in top

Aug. 22, 2010: Coaches meet at midfield before Nebraska football practice in Lincoln. From left: Joe Moglia, Shawn Watson, Jeff Jamrog and Bo Pelini.

gun capacity. Again, nothing wrong with that. Pelini's job isn't to surround himself with Husker heroes. His job is to win. He has to feel good about the way he does that.

There are probably some Husker fans disappointed in Pelini today. But put it this way: If we weren't talking about Scott Frost, a young coach with just two years experience at Oregon wouldn't even be in the conversation for the job that isn't open yet.

3. It could very well be that the time is not right for the Frost/Nebraska fairy tale ending. Could

that time come again? Absolutely. But I wonder if Frost isn't missing a keen opportunity here, not only to be on the ground level of Pelini's offense, but to join Pelini's inner circle. What if Pelini stays here 10 years, 15 years? What if Tim Beck has big success and leaves to become a head coach? Would Frost have a better chance at the Husker offensive coordinator job one day if he had been here and had Pelini's trust?

That's a lot of speculation for a job that's not open. For now, know that both Frost and Pelini are doing what they have to do and it's probably the best for both.

COACHING CAREER: 2002-2017

2002: Nebraska Cornhuskers
Defensive graduate assistant (2002)
2002 Independence Bowl

2006: Kansas State Wildcats
Defensive graduate assistant (2006)

2007-2008: Northern Iowa Panthers
Linebackers coach (2007)
Co-defensive coordinator (2008)

2009-2015: Oregon Ducks
Receivers coach (2009-12)
Offensive coordinator (2013-15)

2016-2017: Central Florida Knights
Head coach

COACHING AWARDS

Oregon
- 2014 Broyles Award Finalist (Nation's Top Assistant)
- 2015 Inducted in Nebraska Football Hall of Fame

Central Florida
- 2017 AAC Coach of the Year
- National Coach of the Year by The Associated Press and the American Football Coaches Association
- Home Depot Coach of the Year
- Paul "Bear" Bryant Coach of the Year
- Eddie Robinson Coach of the Year
- Semifinalist 2016 and 2017, George Munger Coach of the Year

June 21, 2002: Scott gives direction to a group of aspiring players.

FROST CONTINUED TO COME HOME even as his alma mater went a different direction. He was back to speak at a Nebraska Coaches Association clinic in that 2011 summer, giving advice to local high school coaches because he felt a "responsibility" to give back to the state's prep scene. He loved Oregon, he told reporters then, but the song is right: There is no place like Nebraska.

"It would be nice to be back here someday," Frost said. "This is my home. I have a lot of friends here. I'm really passionate about this program."

Frost and Nebraska again found themselves linked in December 2014 after Athletic Director Shawn Eichorst fired Pelini following seven seasons. Mike Bellotti — the man who hired Frost at Oregon and had become an ESPN analyst — recommended the Huskers hire their former quarterback during a live broadcast.

A Las Vegas sportsbook even tabbed Frost as the favorite for the job at 5-2 odds. Nebraska's eventual hire — Oregon State coach Mike Riley — was not part of the list.

But there was no chance Husker fans would give up on the hope of Frost one day coming home for good.

Scott, as Oregon's offensive coordinator, is a Broyles Award finalist in 2014. The award is given annually to the nation's top assistant.

JAN. 11, 2015

NU WOULD BE WISE TO REMAIN ON GOOD TERMS WITH FROST

BY TOM SHATEL

DALLAS — There he sat, with the waves of media crashing into his interview table, unfazed. A most popular man.

Scott Frost, innovator and button-pusher of the most dangerous offense in college football.

Scott Frost, the hottest young coach in the college game and potentially its next great coach.

Perhaps, one day at Nebraska.

But that day was not going to come this year.

In the midst of an hour media opportunity for Monday night's Oregon vs. Ohio State national championship game, Frost was asked if he had any opportunities to become a head coach in the past month.

"I've had chances three years in a row," Frost said. "I love where I am. If I leave, it's going to be for the right one."

Did Nebraska contact you after firing Bo Pelini?

"No," Frost said. "I was never contacted by Nebraska in regards to any position."

Were you surprised NU didn't call?

Frost said no, then declined to comment, other than to add, "I wish Mike Riley the best. I think he's a good coach."

His tone here was matter-of-fact. Frost made it clear he had a lot on his plate this week and preferred not to dive into the career questions on the eve of the national championship game.

Big deal? Frost has an impressive résumé, and the facts are as plain as the Rose Bowl scoreboard on Jan. 1. But he's never been a head coach. In the wake of the inexperience of the last staff, it could be that Nebraska Athletic Director Shawn Eichorst wanted someone who had run his own program. I get that.

Eichorst identified Riley early. He wanted to move fast. This wasn't Frost's time.

Meanwhile, there was no need to call Frost about taking another offensive coordinator job. He's got the best one in college football. Frost's next move will be as head coach.

He was mentioned by Colorado media as a guy who could have had the Colorado State opening. And while CSU is certainly not a bad job, Frost is a smart guy. He knows he can afford to be patient. He can sit up in that play-calling booth, surrounded by Oregon riches and talent, and keep building up his brand until a bigger job — one less risky — comes along. New Pitt coach Pat Narduzzi did that.

Whenever he jumps, Frost is someone Nebraskans will surely keep an eye on. And make no mistake, this is someone the school should keep a good relationship with. His allegiance to his school and state is well-known. On Saturday, after talking about the list of hall of fame coaches he's been exposed to, Frost added that Tom Osborne "is my hero."

Could Nebraska one day be in a similar position to Michigan, which had the good fortune of having one of its alumni grow up to be one of the best coaches on the planet? You never know.

For now, the son of two coaches — Larry and Carol Frost — from Wood River, Neb., finds it ironic that he's even here, taking the questions and looking the part of the bright young coach.

"I never wanted to coach, to be honest with you," Frost said. "I learned a lot from my parents, who were both coaches. Most of my career, I saw the hours coaches kept and I thought they were crazy.

"I used to watch guys sleep in their office and thought they were out of their mind. But once I was out of the game, I missed it too much."

That was in 2004.

It worked for three years, and Frost had stops at Cleveland, Green Bay and Tampa Bay, when Bucs defensive coaches Raheem Morris and Mike Tomlin (now Pittsburgh Steeler head coach) talked Frost into the coaching life.

Now, Frost says, he loves it. Ever sleep in your office?

"No," he said. "Not intentionally."

Wasn't it just yesterday that Frost went on national TV and stumped for Osborne to win a national championship after that final game against Tennessee?

Frost is back in the spotlight in the national championship arena. He's seasoned, but he's still a no-nonsense leader. During his hour of interviews, he was polite and gracious but didn't suffer foolish questions. He chided one writer for continuing to probe about Oregon receiver Darren Carrington's suspension. When an ESPN reporter said a draft guy at his network questioned whether Ducks quarterback Marcus Mariota would make it in the NFL, Frost said, "Makes me wonder who ESPN is getting for draft experts."

Mostly, they wanted to know about this Oregon offense that has taken on almost mythical life, how the machine works and how this former Nebraska quarterback decides how fast to drive it.

"It's a feel thing," Frost said. "It's easy to see from the box when another team is getting tired, how they're lining up. You kind of have to balance that with how your team is feeling and executing. You don't want to leave your defense on the field too long. We've been smarter with that this year, trying to pick our spots instead of putting our foot on the gas the whole time."

Someone tried to compare the Oregon and Ohio State offenses, and Frost wouldn't have it, saying Oregon was different from Ohio State or "Nebraska, Arizona or Arizona State or any other spreads."

Nebraska. There's that name again.

Oregon's offense runs on rocket fuel, and Frost's career track could hit warp speed if he pushes the buttons to a national title Monday night. But that's for later. Any other questions. Oh, here comes a radio guy with one.

"Scott, you had a big day a couple of days ago, the big 4-0 (40th birthday)," said the radio guy. "Am I right about that?"

Frost: "Yeah, thanks for bringing that up."

"Did you do anything to celebrate? Did your wife do anything special?"

Frost: "Well, I don't have a wife, and I worked all day."

The news there is that the kid from Wood River is 40. How did that happen? We're all getting older. Meanwhile, Frost keeps getting better.

FROST'S CONNECTIONS

 1993-94
Stanford
Cardinal

 1998-00
New York
Jets

 2001
Cleveland
Browns

 2001-02
Green Bay
Packers

 2003
San Francisco
49ers

Bill Walsh
Head coach

Bill Parcells
Head coach

Butch Davis
Head coach

Mike Sherman
Head coach

Jim Mora
Defensive coordinator

Bill Belichick
Defensive coordinator

Chuck Pagano
Defensive backs coach

Bo Pelini
Linebackers coach

 1995-97
Nebraska
Cornhuskers

Tom Osborne
Head coach

Todd Bowles
Secondary coach

Brett Favre
Quarterback

Keyshawn Johnson
Receiver

Ahman Green
Running back
(and former Husker)

2003-04
Tampa Bay
Buccaneers

 2006
Kansas State
Wildcats

 2007-08
Northern Iowa
Panthers

 2009-15
Oregon
Ducks

Jon Gruden
Head coach

John Lynch
Nine-time
Pro Bowl safety

Ron Prince
Head coach

Mark Farley
Head coach

Chip Kelly
Head coach

Mike Tomlin
Defensive backs/
secondary coach

Ronde Barber
Five-time
Pro-Bowl defensive back

Raheem Morris
Defensive coordinator

Mario Verduzco
Co-offensive coordinator/
quarterbacks coach
*(Current NU quarterbacks
coach)*

Mark Helfrich
Head coach

Monte Kiffin
Defensive coordinator

James Franklin
Offensive coordinator

Erik Chinander
Tight ends coach
*(Current NU defensive
coordinator)*

"I'M REALLY NOT SURPRISED AT THE LEVEL OF SUCCESS THAT HE HAS HAD BECAUSE OF THOSE NATURAL INNATE SKILLS THAT HE HAS THAT AREN'T NECESSARILY TAUGHT, THEY ARE GOD-GIVEN."

—MIKE TOMLIN, PITTSBURGH STEELERS HEAD COACH

*Dec. 3, 2017: Scott is introduced as
Nebraska's head coach during a press
conference at Memorial Stadium.*

COMING HOME

2015 TO TODAY

BY SAM MCKEWON

SCOTT FROST HAS A CHISELED, stoic face. He squints when he smiles. It's a face made for hot sunny days when winds blast across the Nebraska Plains he once called home, but it can be hard to read his emotions. His inscrutable expression holds back enough that his frank, direct words, seasoned with light humor, land with a surprising edge.

And so it was no particular surprise when, in the first hours back home — Sunday, Dec. 3, 2017, after he'd just been hired as Nebraska's 30th football coach — Frost did not betray much emotion on the third floor of Memorial Stadium. He smiled at the right moments and played to the crowd when suggesting the Big Ten would have to adjust itself to him, not the other way around. When directly asked about his emotions, he volleyed it back with dry wit.

"I think that's capped it all off, by you asking that question," Frost said.

He wore a sharp silver suit and a loosely-knotted tie. He sat at a table — flanked by helmets bearing No. 7, his old number —

instead of standing at a podium. His new boss, Athletic Director Bill Moos, spoke first. Frost, possessing a vast memory and understanding of the fractured dynamics that bedeviled Husker football for nearly two decades, then answered 30 minutes of questions with no hesitation or notes.

But, in the 20 seconds between Moos' introduction and Frost's opening statement, the magnitude of the moment hit the native son. Moos shook Frost's hand, and, the noise rising around him — ex-teammates in a roar, spectators from a floor above clapping — caused Frost to draw his own hand to his face.

As he glanced around the room, he drew his lips tight.

That's how Nebraskans show they're overcome.

In the middle of those 20 seconds, he found the microphone and choked out a "thank you."

Later, Frost would say he was out of emotions. The whirlwind 48 hours that preceded his introduction were unlike any he'd ever experienced.

FROST HAD KNOWN, for almost a week, he was going to become Nebraska's new head coach. But he'd had the briefest of second thoughts Friday night, talked through those with his old coach and mentor, Tom Osborne, then prepared to win a conference title game with his team, the University of Central Florida. After a thrilling overtime win over Memphis on Central Florida's home field, Frost wept, briefly encountered his parents, Larry and Carol, and eventually told his team the news. He boarded a plane with a handful of staff members and coaches bound for Lincoln. The plane landed after midnight — reporters lining the fence trying to get a peek. Frost got a few hours of sleep, met with his new team, put on that sharp suit, saw Osborne again and reconnected with Matt Davison, the man who caught his most famous pass.

Dec. 2, 2017: Scott celebrates with Central Florida players following the Knights' double-overtime victory over Memphis to win the American Athletic Conference football championship at Spectrum Stadium in Orlando.

He was led to Nebraska's weight room, where ex-teammates and lettermen, awaited. The surprise had been hatched by Moos fewer than 24 hours before, and when Frost saw the Huskers, current and former, he smiled and threw his fists above his head.

"Thanks for coming boys! Let's get this thing right!" Frost said. "Can't believe it!"

He told them he needed their help to make Nebraska "what it is" and he wanted their ideas — except for the bad ones.

"You guys made this place special and I want to get it there again," Frost said.

Throughout that Sunday, Frost made repeated references to the past.

His own past of growing up in the state, growing up on Nebraska's campus, where his mom was coaching track while he was "getting into trouble and getting run over on the Devaney Center track."

Nebraska's now-distant past — a generation ago — of winning conference and national championships.

And, most pointedly, he addressed Nebraska's recent past on the football field.

As Frost's trajectory raced upward over two years that brought him and his alma mater back together, Nebraska's own arc plunged downward until the two crossed paths, Frost eclipsing NU as he rose and the Huskers hurtled to the basement.

"It didn't look like the Nebraska that I knew," Frost said and has said in so many different ways since.

The story of Frost's homecoming is also the story about the decline of Nebraska's football empire, ensnared by its own internal failures, lost in a new league unfazed by the Huskers' history. It is the story of what Frost has come to rescue, a program far enough off its axis that Frost, in a moment of doubt, genuinely considered not taking the job made for him.

The firings of four coaches — Frank Solich, Bill Callahan, Bo Pelini and Mike Riley — and the feuds that ensued from them. Furious fans fleeing the scene of another blowout loss at Memorial Stadium. The tirades, the throat slash, the hat swipe. The revolving door of coaches and administrators. Audio tapes, media debates and dueling golf tournaments. Fingers pointed. Thumbs jammed. Secret meetings held. Social media campaigns with cats and California at their center instead of winning. Bowl streaks lost. Winning seasons, too. Native sons leaving to play elsewhere while the players who remained were pushed around by other Midwestern teams who were tougher, more physical and more motivated. Blackshirts soft as pats of butter. Another team in red, Wisconsin, taking Nebraska's blueprint and making its own wrecking ball that annually cracks Big Red bones.

Nebraska had won 182 games and one Big 12 title since Frost last quarterbacked the Huskers. It played for four more conference crowns, sold out every game, produced Heisman winner Eric Crouch and one of the most-decorated defensive players in college football history with Ndamukong Suh. It moved to the Big Ten, a league that most — even Osborne — believe is best for Nebraska's long-term future. So the Huskers are not exactly Kansas or Iowa State or Minnesota. But as Frost aims to restore the program to its former glory, there is a moment, just before his first season, to recall how Nebraska lost its way just as the native son rises to heal a broken state.

"When I was here under Coach Osborne, there was unity in purpose, and unity in belief, and unity of understanding and unity of support for this program, what it stood for, and what it was accomplishing," Frost said. "This program needs that again, this state needs that again, and when I walked into that weight room and saw all those players there, it really made me excited about the fact that we can get this entire state behind this football program."

The man who watched it up close, who Frost leaned on in an uncertain moment, couldn't have agreed more.

"It's really hard to explain to somebody," Osborne said as he watched Frost talk to his former players. "I mean, we can talk to the coaches that have been here recently, but they never did really understand."

Oct. 8, 2009: Husker Ndamukong Suh sacks Missouri quarterback Blaine Gabbert. Suh, one of the most decorated defensive players in college football history, was a bright spot for Nebraska since Frost last quarterbacked the team.

JOE DAILEY WAS A cultured guy for a quarterback. He read Sun Tzu's "The Art of War." He also ran out of bounds on a fourth-down play to seal a stunning loss to Southern Mississippi, but it's worth noting that, at the end of his final game as a Husker — six full years into the decline — he described where NU football had been, and where it was going for many years to come.

"The way I see this is that great empires, they fall," Dailey said after a 26-20 loss to Colorado. This was 2004, Year One of Callahan, which marked the end of a 35-year streak of bowl games. "Great leaders, they fall. And great college football teams, they fall. Sometimes you need to start over again in order to really appreciate what happened in the past."

And start over again. And again. And again. And, now, again.

Dailey was among the Huskers who straddled the end of Solich's coaching tenure and the beginning of Callahan's four-year stint. His words — even Callahan's ill-fated tenure — seem quaint now. In 2004, Nebraska was three years removed from playing for the national title, five years removed from winning the Big 12 and seven years removed from the end of a 60-3 run that spanned five years, 1993-97, when NU won three national titles.

Husker football rumbled on the Plains, chewed up smaller and faster teams from the coasts and wrote a chapter in college football history. When dynasties are discussed, '90s Nebraska makes the cut.

Osborne retired at the end of the 1997 season leaving the job to his long-time running backs coach, Solich. Osborne had promised Solich he would, and Solich, who'd never been a head coach or even a full-time play-caller, took the keys of the most powerful program in the sport. In 1998, he'd have to replace Frost at quarterback, two dominant defensive players in Jason Peter and Grant Wistrom, Outland Trophy winner Aaron Taylor and one of the best running backs he'd ever coached, Ahman Green. Based on the strength of a spectacular 91-yard touchdown run in the spring game, Bobby Newcombe had

won the job to replace Frost and Nebraska started that season ranked fourth nationally.

"You figure they continue to win at least nine games and conference championships," Omaha World-Herald columnist Tom Shatel wrote on the eve of Solich's first game against Louisiana Tech. "You figure they still cash in their share of blue chips at the recruiting table. What you don't know is the kind of chemistry Solich will mix up and how the team will react to him. Or if Nebraska can really be that lucky to find another coaching legend in-house. Or that maybe the real reason they got all these great players is that Osborne had this secret stand-up comedy routine he would do in recruits' homes. Will Solich have the same delivery? Will Solich deliver?

Aug. 29, 1998: Bobby Newcombe talks to coach Frank Solich in the first half against Louisiana Tech. It was Solich's first game, and first win, as the Nebraska coach.

"You darn well know he will. Because this is Nebraska, and this is what Nebraska does. Somebody once said it couldn't go on forever, but that was back in 1979 or something, and that person is still waiting tables at the Stillwater Holiday Inn."

Solich — a trim, intense-but-friendly everyman who once was a high school driving instructor — didn't guarantee it.

> "A LOT OF PEOPLE SAY IT WILL AUTOMATICALLY KEEP GOING. THAT THE WINS WILL ALWAYS BE THERE. THE WINS WILL BE THERE IF YOU RECRUIT WELL, PREPARE THEM WELL AND DO A GOOD JOB AS A STAFF. TO SAY IT WILL AUTOMATICALLY HAPPEN, THERE'S NO QUESTION THAT REMAINS TO BE SEEN."
>
> — FRANK SOLICH

"A lot of people say it will automatically keep going," Solich said. "That the wins will always be there. The wins will be there if you recruit well, prepare them well and do a good job as a staff. To say it will automatically happen, there's no question that remains to be seen."

Nebraska gave up 590 passing yards — and lost Newcombe to injury for a few games — in Solich's debut, a 56-27 win. It was a sloppy harbinger of a frustrating, injury-riddled season to come.

By October, Nebraska had risen to No. 2, but it lost its first conference game since 1992 with a 28-21 loss at Texas A&M.

"Anytime Nebraska loses," Shatel wrote after the game, "it's front-page news, worldwide."

Two weeks later, there was worldwide front-page news again. Nebraska lost its home winning streak — which stretched longer than seven years — in a 20-16 loss to nemesis Texas and Heisman Trophy winner Ricky Williams.

"I'd have to say it's the lowest point of my athletic career," defensive end Chad Kelsay said.

Nov. 14, 1998: Nebraska quarterback Eric Crouch gets his head whipped around as he is brought down by Kansas State's Travis Ochs in Manhattan. No flag was thrown. Nebraska lost to Kansas State, 40-30, for the first time in 30 years.

Two weeks later, Nebraska lost to Kansas State for the first time in 30 years, with referees missing quarterback Eric Crouch's facemask being twisted 90 degrees on a key fourth-down play.

"The last time we lost to these guys, none of us were even born," tight end Sheldon Jackson said. "This is just one year. We have a lot of new guys, some guys who haven't learned how to win yet. The torch being passed? I'm not falling for that. I don't believe it."

KSU's Bill Snyder would beat Nebraska again in 2000, 2002, 2003 and 2004.

Nebraska finished 9-4, NU's first four-loss season since 1968. The Huskers lost more games in Solich's first year than they did in Osborne's last five. And words spoken by players and coaches that season — shock, anger, denial, certitude it would improve — would be echoed over the next 19 years.

In 1999 — despite a quarterback controversy between Newcombe and Crouch and a star running back, DeAngelo Evans, leaving the team in a huff — Solich coached a powerhouse, the last of the great Husker teams, a 12-1 squad whose only loss was a mistake-filled upset at Texas.

Nebraska avenged that loss in the Big 12 title game, beating the Longhorns for the only time in NU's 15 years in the Big 12, and handily won the Fiesta Bowl over Tennessee. That same night, Nebraska's long-time defensive coordinator, Charlie McBride — who stood shoulder-to-shoulder with Osborne during the Huskers' national title run — announced his retirement.

"I love this football team, and I also love my family very much," McBride said. "It's time for them, so I'm going to pull the plug."

That night, in a tent just outside Sun Devil Stadium, was the peak of the Solich era — and Nebraska football, frankly, since Frost left as quarterback and Osborne retired.

The downside of the mountain initially had a gentle slope. Behind Crouch and a still-powerful rush offense, Nebraska was No. 1 for much of the 2000 season until losses to eventual national champion Oklahoma and Kansas State on a cold, snowy night in Manhattan, Wildcat players celebrating by making snow angels. In 2001 — when Crouch won the Heisman Trophy — Nebraska won its first 11 games before playing rival Colorado in its typical Black Friday slot. CU had its best team in years and had lost its five previous games to Nebraska by 5, 3, 2, 3 and 2 points.

"I LOVE THIS FOOTBALL TEAM, AND I ALSO LOVE MY FAMILY VERY MUCH. IT'S TIME FOR THEM, SO I'M GOING TO PULL THE PLUG."

— CHARLIE MCBRIDE, DEFENSIVE COORDINATOR WHO RETIRED IN 1999

Oct. 27, 2001: Eric Crouch catches a 63-yard touchdown pass from Mike Stuntz in front of Oklahoma's Kory Klein. Crouch's efforts that season earned him the Heisman Trophy.

On Nov. 23, 2001 — the Day After Thanksgiving Massacre — the dam broke. Colorado scored 62 points — the most ever allowed by the Huskers at the time — quickly putting Nebraska in a 35-3 hole. Colorado cracked wide open Nebraska's reputation as the most physical team on the field, running basic counter and zone plays into the Blackshirts' front seven.

"Solich and the Huskers are in deep trouble!" ABC broadcaster Brent Musburger bellowed at one point during the barrage.

"This is a big shock," Crouch said of the 62-36 decimation. "It's tough to talk about because this never happens to us."

Until, in a sense, it happened again in the BCS national title game a month later in the Rose Bowl. There, Miami — so stuffed with talent that many pundits put it alongside 1995 Nebraska as the sport's greatest teams — put Nebraska in a 34-0 hole by halftime before showing some mercy in a 37-14 win.

"Miami would have beaten anyone," tight end Tracey Wistrom said.

Maybe. But Nebraska was moving far closer to being "anyone" than its coaches, players and fans realized.

Nov. 24, 2001: Colorado running back Bobby Purify runs away from Nebraska defenders. Colorado scored 62 points, the most ever allowed by the Huskers at the time.

IN APRIL 2001, Harvey Perlman, a longtime dean of Nebraska's College of Law, became the University of Nebraska-Lincoln's full-time chancellor. He'd been in the interim role since 2000 but, by 2001, it was his, and he would hold the role for 15 years before stepping down in 2016.

He presided, then, over the roughest stretch of Husker football since the miserable 1940s and '50s, when Nebraska had four winning seasons in two decades. And more than a few fans point to the dry-witted, analytical Perlman, and a series of decisions that went sideways, as a culprit of the mediocrity.

"I'm very disappointed in how football transpired over the course of my being chancellor," Perlman said in an interview for this book. He's a professor again in the College of Law. "And if there's anything I could have done to do it better, I wish I would have done it. But I don't know what it was."

Perlman's first big decision came after Solich's worst season in 2002, a shattering 7-7 campaign that left Huskers calling out their teammates. The stunning nature of that season has been lost to time thanks to seasons even worse. But Nebraska's full-bore decline began there. And Solich was seen as one source of the problem. A poll commissioned by The World-Herald in the middle of that season had Solich's job approval at 53 percent — down from 86 percent just two years before.

"I'M VERY DISAPPOINTED IN HOW FOOTBALL TRANSPIRED OVER THE COURSE OF MY BEING CHANCELLOR. AND IF THERE'S ANYTHING I COULD HAVE DONE TO DO IT BETTER, I WISH I WOULD HAVE DONE IT. BUT I DON'T KNOW WHAT IT WAS."

— HARVEY PERLMAN WHO BECAME THE UNIVERSITY OF NEBRASKA-LINCOLN'S FULL-TIME CHANCELLOR IN 2001

Struggles in quarterback recruiting left him with few options beyond rawhide-tough Jammal Lord, a skilled runner who never missed a start but threw more career interceptions than touchdowns. After the late-season collapse in 2001, Solich also opted to keep his defensive coordinator, Craig Bohl, a decision that blew up in Nebraska's face, starting with a 40-7 loss at Penn State.

"It was almost like they knew what defensive coverages we were running," safety Philip Bland said after that game.

By that point in Solich's career, a pattern had emerged. Nebraska was awful on the road against ranked teams. One week after Penn State, Iowa State beat Nebraska like a drum 36-14, the Huskers wearing their Solich-approved all-white uniforms, a red gusset running down the side, giving the look of a bleed out from the pounds of flesh teams kept taking out of the Huskers. Nebraska lost to Oklahoma State, Colorado and ranked Texas when Solich opted to go for the win instead of a game-tying field goal. Lord threw an interception. At Kansas State — a 49-13 loss in which Snyder not-so-subtly ran up the score — Husker center John Garrison had had enough.

"It's pretty obvious that by the end of the game, the score, that they flat out wanted it more," Garrison said. "The heart of this team ... I question it after this game. It's disappointing, it's not

Nebraska football, and it's not this team, either."

Solich fired Bohl and several other defensive assistants. He fired himself as play-caller. Two Husker offensive line coaching legends — Milt Tenopir and Dan Young — retired. In Bohl's place, Solich picked a fiery NFL assistant to coordinate Nebraska's defense. Bo Pelini.

Meanwhile, Perlman was picking an athletic director to replace Bill Byrne, who had left for Texas A&M. An obvious candidate emerged: Steve Pederson, one of Osborne's recruiting coordinators in the 1980s. He was a successful A.D. at Pittsburgh for several years; he had stints at Tennessee and Ohio State; his father was a state senator; he grew up in North Platte, a native son.

"Today, I make a pledge to you," Pederson said then. "With your continued support behind this program — 1.7 million and more playing as one — that whoever wants to take on the Huskers had better bring their 'A' game."

It seemed the perfect fit.

"I don't think the Nebraska fan base was ever as unified and excited about an appointment — other than Scott Frost — than they were with Steve Pederson," Perlman says now.

Pederson spent 19 of his first 26 hours in Lincoln working.

"I'm a little impatient," Pederson said in January 2003. "Oftentimes, I don't understand why everybody doesn't approach things with the same intensity that I do. I generally want things done yesterday."

Pederson said he'd be "hands on" with the football program, not a caretaker. And he had blunt words for his own athletic department, too.

"I sense that we're feeling sorry for ourselves a little bit," Pederson said. "I understand I'm coming in at a time where we've come off a tough football season and the athletic director left. Maybe it's human nature to be down a little bit. But we can't afford that. We just can't afford it, and I'm not going to allow it."

In the same month Pederson and Pelini were hired, Nebraska invited back an injured NFL defensive back to help the Husker defense prepare for the Independence Bowl. Scott Frost had learned a lot about defense in his five-year NFL career, and he applied it to bowl prep. And though Frost hadn't coached the team during the season, he was outspoken about his desire that NU stay the course.

"The resources in this state and the elements in this state all lend themselves to playing the kind of football we've been playing here," Frost said. "People screaming for radical change are overreacting."

Dec. 27, 2002: A frustrated Frank Solich hits the turf after a flag was waved off in the fourth quarter of Nebraska's loss to Ole Miss in the Independence Bowl. Fan attendance was light.

Nov. 30, 2003: Husker football player Benard Thomas asks a question of Athletic Director Steve Pederson during a press conference announcing the firing of Frank Solich.

THE PILOTS LAUGHED as they came off the Cessna S550 turbojet at Millard Airport. They were alone, and that's part of the punchline.

"All we were told to do was to fly to Fayetteville and pick him up," one pilot said.

Fayetteville, Arkansas, that is. To pick up Steve Pederson's high-priced Hail Mary pass, Arkansas coach Houston Nutt, one of the many men who said no to replacing Frank Solich.

"You don't send a corporate jet like this all that way unless you think that you are going to bring somebody back," the pilot said. "But if we did bring him back, we would have landed in Lincoln. Not here."

This was more than a month into a search that stripped the emperor of all his clothes. A mystery coach Perlman insists was interested said no. Dave Wannstedt — who later worked for Pederson at Pittsburgh — said no. A Kansas City Chiefs offensive coordinator said no. A Philadelphia Eagles offensive coordinator said no. A Dallas defensive coordinator said no. And, of course, Nutt said no, with the amount of money — Nutt said in an unrelated lawsuit deposition that NU offered $2 million, though Pederson repeatedly denied it — a source of controversy for months afterward.

"Embarrassing," Perlman says now. "Airplanes sitting on tarmacs."

There are consequences to firing a coach who finished 58-19 in six years. Pederson did it, axing Solich on Saturday night after a 9-3 season, after he was given a Gatorade bath for a road win at Colorado. The day after the firing, players fumed in the back of Pederson's press conference to announce Solich's firing. One, Benard Thomas, even fired off some questions. Pederson was steadfast.

"I refuse to let this program gravitate to mediocrity," Pederson said. "We will not surrender the Big 12 Conference to Oklahoma and Texas."

FIRING ENDS SOLICH ERA

BY RICH KAIPUST AND ELIZABETH MERRILL

One day after he got a Gatorade bath in an emotional win at Colorado, Nebraska Coach Frank Solich was fired Saturday night during a five-minute meeting with Athletic Director Steve Pederson.

Assistant Coach Marvin Sanders said Solich called staff members late Saturday and told them that his termination would be immediate.

NU Defensive Coordinator Bo Pelini will be named interim head coach, people within the program said. The staff, minus Solich, will coach the Huskers through the bowl game.

Nebraska completed its regular season at 9-3 with a 31-22 win at Colorado on Friday. The Huskers are awaiting their bowl assignment, with the Dec. 30 Holiday Bowl in San Diego being the likely destination.

Saturday marked the first time Nebraska has fired a head football coach since Bill Jennings in 1961.

Neither Solich nor Pederson could be reached Saturday night.

But people close to the program said Solich met Pederson at South Stadium at 7:30 p.m., and the first-year athletic director asked the coach if he would resign. Solich, who said all last week that he wouldn't step down, didn't budge.

Pederson then fired him, according to at least three people who had talked to Solich.

It's the second consecutive offseason purge at a program that was once praised nationally for its continuity. After last year's 7-7 season, Solich fired three assistants and hired six new coaches.

Nov. 28, 2003: Frank Solich gets animated on the sidelines in the first half of Nebraska's win over Colorado, 31-22. He was fired the next day after a 9-3 season.

People close to Solich said the sixth-year coach assumed he'd have at least two years with his new staff. On Friday, after the win in Boulder, several players made public pleas to Pederson to keep the staff.

Bob Sawdon, a friend of Solich's, said the 59-year-old coach was disappointed and stunned by Pederson's decision.

"I just think Pederson came in here with an agenda," Sawdon said. "This is going to set Nebraska football back 10 years, believe me.

"I can't believe somebody won't pick up the sixth (winningest) coach in the country. And I think it will come back to haunt Nebraska. This program's going to go south for a while."

PEDERSON'S DECISION, made after just 11 months on the job, split the state.

"It's horrible and unprofessional. That's not Nebraska football," one Husker fan said in an Omaha World-Herald story.

"Maybe now we can get back to playing some real football," another said.

"It's all politics," said a third. "The boosters and athletic director were going to do whatever it took to get him out of there."

In some ways, the program never recovered. For some, almost nothing can undo the wrong done to Solich. Not Pederson's eventual firing. Not Osborne's eventual return to the athletic director chair. Not Pelini's ascension to the head job. Perhaps only Frost's return — and the new coach has spoken often and fondly of Solich already — can fully heal the wound.

The backlash Pederson faced was immediate and swift. One fan mailed his Nebraska hat to the university president, saying he could no longer wear it. Talk radio callers debated. Near the conclusion of Pederson's search — which ended with the hiring of Callahan — a white pickup zoomed by his office window.

In the bed of the truck, according to an Omaha World-Herald story, was a 6-foot sign that said, "Fire NU's A.D. now. Ask us How."

The perfect hire — Pederson — helped create a perfect storm that's never really stopped swirling around the program.

Pederson rebuffed the popular choice at the time — Pelini, who had coached the team to a win in the Alamo Bowl, to Husker fan cheers of "We Want Bo!" — and kept cycling through NFL options until one fell in his lap. Callahan was newly fired from the Oakland Raiders, was the son of a Chicago cop. He'd coached — and lost — in the Super Bowl. He'd been in the college game as an offensive line coach. He was steeped in the art of the West Coast offense, which hadn't lost much of its shine in 12 years between when Frost picked Stanford and Callahan arrived in Lincoln.

"Nebraska fans have wanted to see the ball in the air more for a long time, and he'll probably give them a chance to see that happen," Osborne said shortly after Callahan was hired.

"I don't think you come in and you jam a system down anybody's throat," Callahan said the day he was hired. "I'll need to sit down and assess and evaluate last year's film. I think that's critical before we make any decisions as to where this offense is going to go."

Callahan was a workaholic. Cerebral, organized, a little aloof, he prized recruiting down to the smallest detail of a player's hand measurements. He signed three quarterbacks in his first recruiting class — the least-heralded, Joe Ganz, actually posted one of the best seasons in Husker history in 2008 — and immediately began piecing together what would become one of the top recruiting classes in the nation in 2005. Callahan consistently scouted, lured and signed players who looked the part and, for a brief time — after he'd been fired — those players coalesced into something that almost resembled what Nebraska had been.

But recruiting was the silver lining to a dark, frustrating four years of Nebraska football. Callahan did, in fact, force the West Coast offense down the throat of his team despite not having a quarterback on the roster who could handle it at the time. He axed most of Solich's assistants — a common practice now, but shocking for NU fans at the time — watered down the walk-on program, and had a manner that suggested all the losing that happened in his first season, when Nebraska finished 5-6, was a phase.

"It's one game today, one season," Callahan said when NU's bowl streak was snapped.

It was more than that.

It was a 70-10 loss at Texas Tech made that way by Callahan's dogged stubbornness to have a true freshman quarterback — Beau Davis — relieve Dailey and repeatedly throw the ball when Nebraska had no chance of coming back. Davis completed five passes — four to the other team.

Oct. 9, 2004: Nebraska's Seppo Evwaraye watches the big screen from the sidelines late in the fourth quarter as Texas Tech wraps up a 70-10 shellacking of Nebraska in Lubbock.

Oct. 29, 2005: Bill Callahan completes what appears to be a slashing motion across his throat directed toward referees in a loss to Oklahoma.

Dec. 28, 2005: Athletic Director Steve Pederson congratulates Bill Callahan after Nebraska beat Michigan, 32-28, in the Alamo Bowl.

It was a 40-15 loss in 2005 at Kansas that even Callahan had to admit was "God-awful." It was a throat slash he made toward referees in a 2005 loss to Oklahoma — one year after calling Sooner fans "hillbillies" — and his strange rationalization of it.

"I did make a gesture out of frustration, which I normally have done with my own children when I've had it up to here," Callahan said.

The peaks — a 30-3 win at Colorado in 2005 that had Pederson beaming like a proud papa, a bowl win over Michigan, quarterback Zac Taylor's Big 12 Offensive Player of the Year Award in 2006, punctuated by a game-winning drive at Texas A&M — were balanced with valleys over Callahan's first three years.

The 2006 Huskers reached the Big 12 title game but lost 21-7 to Oklahoma. A distraught, clad-in-black Callahan declared himself "just sick, really sick" about it on his TV show. Then came a Cotton Bowl loss to Auburn. It set up 2007, when Callahan would have flashy transfer quarterback Sam Keller and the majority of a strong 2006 defense back.

Every moment in Callahan's Nebraska tenure led up to — and away from — the third game of NU's 2007 season, when USC, the first No. 1 team to play at Memorial Stadium since 1978, came to town.

ESPN's "College GameDay" was there. A packed press box leaned in. One Los Angeles Times columnist spent the entire week in Nebraska for a series of stories. A national TV audience waited to see: Had Callahan really pulled Husker football off the canvas?

No. USC gained 8.2 yards per carry and led 42-10 before cruising to a 49-31 win.

"We had a lot of room to run," USC coach Pete Carroll said.

Pederson had given Callahan a contract extension two weeks before the USC loss. Perlman himself had given Pederson a five-year contract extension that summer.

"We'll be hitting on all cylinders," Pederson said at the time of his contract extension.

Neither made it to winter.

> "YOU THINK IT JUST ENDS ON THE FIELD WITH THE FANS? NO, IT DOESN'T END THERE. IT DOESN'T END ANYWHERE. IT'S HARD FOR ME TO GO TO CLASS AFTER PLAYING THE WAY I PLAYED. IT'S HARD FOR ME TO SIT THERE AND KNOW THAT EVERYONE AROUND ME IS LOOKING AT ME THINKING SOMETHING."
>
> — FORMER NEBRASKA LINEBACKER COREY MCKEON, IN 2007 AFTER NEBRASKA NEARLY LOST TO BALL STATE

Nov. 23, 2007: Fans share their opinions at the game against Colorado at Folsom Field.

A PRIZEFIGHTER BELIEVING he'd scored the most stunning upset, he held both arms up, like a champ, with the playsheet that had delivered this win clutched hard in his right hand. Nebraska had won another conference title, it seemed. The Huskers were back, all the way back, with a tough-talking, hard-edged defensive coach who reminded some of Bob Devaney. He was so different from the man who hired him, Tom Osborne, that it was the perfect odd couple, because he could brashly say all the things modest Midwesterners felt but declined to express in polite company. He could — and did — call referees names. He could — and did — put reporters in their place. He could — and did — pump his fist and twist up his face and live every second of a Husker football game the way fans could. And if you didn't like it, tough. He didn't need you anyway. He was the Big Red id, and if he could win, he could control it enough to become a Cornhusker cult hero. He even had the name for it: Bo.

For one second, Bo Pelini had thrust up his arms in a 12-10 victory over Texas in the 2009 Big 12 championship game. Then he brought them back down in shock and confusion. Officials were huddling. The game wasn't over. UT's quarterback, Colt McCoy had thrown a pass that landed out of bounds with time still on the clock.

"The previous play is under further review."

One second was going back on the clock, and the hated Longhorns got to attempt a game-winning field goal. Texas made the kick, and the dream was pulled away to reveal a nightmare.

"BCS!" Pelini shouted as he entered the locker room. "That's why they make that call!"

As chronicled by The World-Herald's Dirk Chatelain in a story on the moments after the loss, this was peak Bo, unleashed and upset, suggesting the Big 12, in that moment, made a conspiratorial decision to give Texas the extra second so the Longhorns could play Alabama for the Bowl Championship Series national title in the Rose Bowl. If inspired stretches of football were one hallmark of the Pelini era, so, were fits of

Dec. 5, 2009: Ndamukong Suh sacks Texas quarterback Colt McCoy in the second quarter in the Big 12 Championship game at Cowboys Stadium in Arlington, Texas. The Longhorns kicked a last-second field goal to win.

paranoia. Pelini demanded to see anyone he could that night — Osborne, Big 12 Commissioner Dan Beebe, Big 12 head of officiating Walt Anderson.

"I want an explanation!" Pelini yelled outside his locker room.

No explanation — however reasonable — could have satisfied him or Husker fans. Pelini's tenure at Nebraska could be its own drama-filled book. His most-famous tirades live on in Internet videos. Now the coach at Youngstown State, he's still video fodder with short-and-blunt press conferences and his rants at referees. He won nine games every season, never got beyond a certain plateau and his teams started to get worse the longer he was in the Big Ten. A man who honestly knew his "black-and-white" nature could grind on people, Pelini increasingly bristled at the expectations that remain in the hearts of most Husker fans — conference and national titles. He also fixated — to a degree that eventually reached his players — on the fractured politics of Nebraska football, ones that started years before, when Solich was summarily booted from the job.

Pelini was there in 2003 for Solich's final season. He had been Solich's best decision as a head coach, as Pelini was a firebrand defensive coordinator who lit a fire under players, who'd in turn run through a wall for him. Several players wanted Pelini as the coach in 2004 when the job had gone to Callahan. Pelini instead went to work for Oklahoma and childhood friend Bob Stoops. Later, he took a job at LSU.

As Callahan's final year at Nebraska went down in flames, Pelini's star was rising at LSU, where he was crafting a national-title winning defense. Juxtaposed against Nebraska's own defense — which gave up 477 yards per game and 76 points in one game, leaving defensive coordinator Kevin Cosgrove literally in tears — Pelini looked like a savior.

Osborne already had been a savior, taking over the A.D. job from Pederson, who was fired after a 45-14 home loss to Oklahoma State that cleared fans out of the stadium in sorrow and anger.

"I've been asked if and when I would ever call for the firing of the athletic director or the football coach," Shatel wrote in his column after the game. "The answer: I don't have to. On the most surreal day in Nebraska football history, Callahan and Co. made that case by themselves Saturday. It was that obvious. It was that sad and depressing."

An omen of what would happen in 2017.

Osborne fired Callahan at the end of the 5-7 season.

"You've got to remember that we went (42) years without a losing season, and now in four years we've had two," Osborne said. "And so the issue becomes, at what point are you still viable?"

To stay viable, Osborne chose Pelini, who'd never been a head coach, over former Husker quarterback and NU assistant Turner Gill, who had. Osborne advised Pelini — and Bo agreed — to keep key parts of Callahan's offensive staff. Offensive coordinator Shawn Watson stayed. So did recruiting coordinator Ted Gilmore. Pelini otherwise surrounded himself with coaches he knew and liked, including his brother, Carl, as defensive coordinator. He kept some of the coaches he'd worked with at Nebraska in 2003. Upon his hiring, he thanked Solich.

"I think what makes the University of Nebraska unique over any place I've been coaching is how much it means to the state," Pelini said. "It's like one big family, and that's what I want us to be."

And for a time — nearly three seasons — the Pelini train rumbled along with a full capacity of Husker fans on board. Nebraska's defense improved immediately under Pelini's tutelage and the Huskers twice played for Big 12 titles. With Osborne in the A.D. chair and the department pulling in the same direction, Pelini generally got a pass from fans when it came to lighting into coaches, reporters or even players.

Oct. 11, 2008: Bo Pelini gives Quentin Castille a mouthful after NU failed to convert on fourth-and-1 late in the second half at Texas Tech.

Nov. 20, 2010: Bo Pelini yells at the officiating crew during the Texas A&M game at Kyle Field. The Huskers were penalized 16 times in the 9-6 loss. Fans questioned whether Pelini could control himself on the sidelines.

The opening five games of the 2010 season — with new, blazingly fast quarterback Taylor Martinez running the option — seemed to suggest Pelini had the goods to close out Nebraska's tenure in the Big 12 with an undefeated season. NU was escaping its old league — especially greedy, autocratic Texas — for the Big Ten, which hadn't had nearly as much of the Big 12's success in the 2000s.

But Nebraska lost — again — to Texas. Again at home. And not to a vintage Texas team, but a bad one. And later that season, the Huskers lost 9-6 at Texas A&M in a game that not only suggested that officials had it in for Pelini and Nebraska

(the Huskers were penalized 16 times) but also, perhaps, that Pelini could no longer control himself on the sidelines. He lit into multiple players — including Martinez in a nose-to-nose yelling session — in a way that left Perlman frustrated enough to respond to a reporter's questions after the game. Pelini's brother, Carl, destroyed a camera on the field after the game. It was a mess only Woody Hayes would have dreamed up.

In a packed press conference the following Monday — administrators sitting in the back — a contrite, evasive Pelini apologized for his actions and brushed off suggestions that Martinez had left the team.

"At times during that game, I got too animated," Pelini said. "I regret that, and I'm sorry about that."

In Nebraska's final game of the Big 12 era, it jumped to a 17-0 lead on Oklahoma in the Big 12 Championship. The Huskers lost 23-20. They then stunk up the Holiday Bowl with a 19-7 loss to Washington, a team they had beaten by 35 points in September.

And, with that, they joined the Big Ten. Nebraska had confidence entering a league that had the reputation of being slower, more methodical, less athletic.

"We just worry about getting us done, working on our stuff," center Mike Caputo said at the time. "And we'll let them adapt to us."

But the league hasn't been kind to Nebraska. Its first game — at Wisconsin, where Husker fans wore black to stand out (and mark themselves for jeers) — was a disaster. The Badgers rolled 48-17. The Huskers have lost 11 games to Big Ten teams by at least 21 points since joining the league, including a 70-31 loss to Wisconsin in the 2012 Big Ten title game when the Huskers seemed confident of reaching the Rose Bowl. Basic running plays bulldozed Bo's D, especially when run by Wisconsin, which has employed three different head coaches since Nebraska joined the league, all of whom own a pummeling win over the Huskers.

Nov. 17, 2010: Bo Pelini walks out of the tunnel with Athletic Director Tom Osborne before the start of the Minnesota game.

DECEMBER 1, 2012

WRECK AT INDY: BADGERS' GROUND GAME RUNS OVER, THROUGH HUSKERS

BY SAM MCKEWON

INDIANAPOLIS — Run over.

Wisconsin's fist of a physical offense — prepared, diverse, focused — popped Nebraska's six-week winning bubble with the swift, blunt force of a Badger toppling an ant hill.

A five-loss team with weeks to plot and house money to burn humbled the Huskers 70-31, nabbed its third straight Rose Bowl berth and pressed the reset button on an NU season that had been defined by improbable, clutch comebacks.

Should those fond memories eventually linger, Saturday night will still live in Husker infamy.

And even if he couldn't explain it, coach Bo Pelini at least grasped the magnitude of this beating. Before he took a question from the media, he apologized for the performance and took the fall for it.

"We came unglued," he said. "I wish I had an answer for it, but I don't. Shock doesn't even begin to explain that. It was like a leaking boat. One thing after another. One problem after another ... I've never been a part of a game like that as a coach. At the end of the day, it falls on me. It falls directly on my shoulders."

The defense gave up 640 total yards — including a school record 539 on the ground — to a third-string quarterback leading a Wisconsin offense ranked 84th nationally. The Badgers led 42-10 at halftime and gained 10.7 yards per play, their running backs acting like hot knives through Blackshirt butter. Three runs longer than 60

yards. Three backs gaining at least 100 yards.

Wisconsin didn't throw a pass in the second half. It scored 28 points.

"What is defensive football?" Pelini asked rhetorically, acidly. "It's play your gaps, handle your responsibility, be where you're supposed to be and make tackles. We did none of the above."

Said safety P.J. Smith: "In this type of defense, when one player messes up, it's going for six. That's exactly what happened tonight. ... We didn't step up to the plate."

Nebraska's offense gained 477 yards and eventually scored 31 points, but played from a 14-0 hole just 2:07 into the game. Quarterback Taylor Martinez had moments of brilliance — a 76-yard touchdown scramble-and-weave that could be his finest run — and three costly turnovers. His first interception was returned for a 29-yard touchdown when it bounced out of Kenny Bell's hands and into Wisconsin cornerback Marcus Cromartie's mitts.

Offensive coordinator Tim Beck said he wasn't even sure when he shifted to Plan B. But Martinez attempted 33 passes, was sacked five times and scrambled several more. So Beck called more than 40 passes in 78 plays.

Hauling the kitchen sink into a half-empty Lucas Oil Stadium, the Badgers surely had something to do with this rout. They ran plays out of a dizzying number of sets, had a wide receiver and a running back throw passes, and designed a pass rush that featured five defenders roaming around before the snap, looking to puncture

holes in Nebraska's confused offensive line.

But mostly, Wisconsin (8-5 overall) crushed the soul of Pelini's defense, running through the overmatched line, around the linebackers and past Husker defensive backs, who repeatedly took poor pursuit angles. Defensive coordinator John Papuchis said UW's plan clearly attacked the flanks of NU's defense — much like UCLA and Ohio State — and it produced even more dramatic results than those two teams did.

"Some of the perimeter stuff was designed to bounce and make us make plays in space," Papuchis said. "Obviously, that's something we struggled with at times this year. And they certainly exposed us today."

In front of 41,260 fans — more of them Huskers than Badgers — UW freshman Melvin Gordon started the fun with a 56-yard end around for a touchdown on the game's fourth play. NU safeties Daimion Stafford and Smith whiffed on tackles. It was harbinger of long runs and gaping holes to come.

Gordon would bust off 24-yard and 60-yard runs later in the first half. In the fourth quarter, with a 39-point lead, Gordon had a 46-yard run on the same end around. He finished with 216 yards — on nine carries.

Montee Ball had a 57-yard touchdown in the third quarter, punctuated by a stiff-arm jab to the face mask of nickel back Ciante Evans. He had 202 yards — on 21 carries. James White had a 68-yard touchdown, zooming through a gaping hole seemingly left over from the Kevin Cosgrove campaign.

Though Pelini insisted otherwise, Nebraska (10-3) felt the loss of defensive tackle Baker Steinkuhler, who hurt his knee last week in a win over Iowa. His replacement, undersized end Cameron Meredith, often found himself blasted four, five, six yards away from the play by Badger linemen double teaming him.

"They controlled us up front, and when they do that, you don't have a chance," Rick Kaczenski said of his whole line, not just Meredith. "You don't have a chance."

Unlike the aftermath of the 2010 Big 12 championship — when Pelini restricted most of his players and assistants from talking — several made their way to a small, square interview room in the stadium's guts. Outside, more milled around eating pizza. The Huskers talked quietly, even thoughtfully, but offered vague insights into how a team so canny at overcoming its mistakes foundered so completely in the biggest game of its collective life — of the entire Pelini era — against a Wisconsin squad it had already beaten in September.

"They played hard," guard Spencer Long said. "They're a physical team, and we didn't match them tonight."

"Normally, I feel like we're unified and we're down to come back, and I can't say what it was, but today felt different," defensive tackle Chase Rome said. "We couldn't get it done. We couldn't pull it out."

"It was a weird game today for some reason," Smith said. "We just didn't do nothing right on defense. Nothing."

Pelini blamed himself. The players blamed themselves. The assistants said no, it was more on them. There was no finger pointing. No Big Ten title rings for those fingers, either.

Dec. 1, 2012: Wisconsin's offense, led by Melvin Gordon's 216 yards on nine carries, shreds the Nebraska defense in the Big Ten Championship game. The Badgers win 70-31 and roll up 640 total yards.

And that was the goal for a team with 29 seniors, who'd vowed to be great, not just good, who'd taken every twist and turn for a six-game winning streak that had Husker fans smelling roses. They came to Indianapolis confident, tight end Kyler Reed said, as confident as they'd been all year. But not too confident. Just right. And a great week of practice. And Pelini said Nebraska prepared for 99 percent of what Wisconsin used Saturday night.

So no alarms. Just surprises.

"We failed," Pelini said. "We failed to win a championship. That was the goal coming in. Didn't get it done."

Said linebacker Will Compton: "As a team, what we sacrificed to get here — that's what hurts the most. That's what hurts the most. This was our championship game. This was it for us. And we blew it."

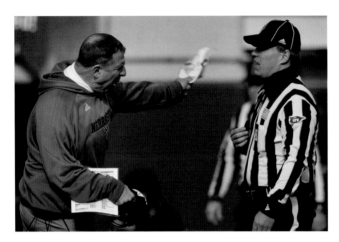

Nov. 29, 2013: Bo Pelini swipes his hat in the direction of linesman Steven Matarante during the Iowa game at Memorial Stadium. Pelini is flagged for the incident.

Though Pelini won far more games than Callahan, the peaks and valleys of his tenure often seemed the same. A win over a ranked Michigan State team would be offset with an upset loss to Northwestern and a blowout loss at Michigan. A hard-fought battle at Penn State was followed by a middling effort against Iowa. A hot, fun night against Miami was balanced against a second-half flop against UCLA. And rarely could Nebraska beat the A-list teams on its schedule. Its 2011 win over Ohio State came against a Buckeye program in transition from Jim Tressel to Urban Meyer. Once Meyer was coach one year later, OSU dropped 63 points on Pelini's defense.

Still, had Pelini's anger not consumed him, he may still be at Nebraska.

"But, I mean, he was Bo," Perlman says now in reference to Osborne taking the chance to hire him. Pelini was volatile. And he made enemies — like the one who, in 2013, sent a secret audiotape, recorded after Nebraska's comeback win over Ohio State in 2011, to sports news website Deadspin. Pelini curses the media and the fans.

"They can all kiss my ass out the (expletive) door," Pelini said on the tape.

"Obviously there was an agenda behind it," Pelini said after the release of the tape.

Perlman says now he thought the moment was bad. But Osborne — who by then had been replaced by Athletic Director Shawn Eichorst — vouched for Pelini, saying he'd already addressed the issue after hearing the tape well before its release. By the end of that season, Pelini suggested Eichorst — a longtime administrator who'd spent many years inside Wisconsin's athletic department — could fire him if he pleased. Eichorst did not. He held firm. Perlman agreed.

"Maybe I should have fired Bo earlier — and just done it on my own — but there were problems with that, too," Perlman says now.

In 2014 — as Frost, at Oregon, was putting together his finest season as an assistant coaching Marcus Mariota to a Heisman Trophy — Pelini was finishing his tenure at Nebraska. The Huskers again won nine games — always consistent there — but lost to ranked foes Michigan State and Wisconsin. In the latter, a 59-24 Badger stomp in light snow, UW running back Melvin Gordon ran for 408 yards … in three quarters.

"Somewhere along the way, it was like our guys totally lost their confidence," Pelini said afterward. One week later, a loss to Minnesota essentially sealed Pelini's fate. After a 37-34 comeback win at Iowa — Pelini's last game was one of his team's patented dramatic escapes — he was fired on a Sunday morning.

"Although we did win a bunch of games, we didn't win the games that mattered the most," Eichorst said. "I think we gave Coach ample time, ample resources and ample support to get that done."

For the second time, the fan base splintered in two. The Bo-lievers against the Bo-leavers. Osborne's second pick, ousted by an A.D. picked by Perlman. In his two years on campus,

Eichorst had not left a strong impression on most people. He was evasive and academic and though he believed in positivity, it had a curious, distant edge to it, as if he held it as a theory. Pelini, already frustrated with critics, chafed most under Eichorst. In a secret meeting held at a local high school days later, Pelini gathered his players and left his most profane rant for last.

Of course, someone recorded it.

Of course, it made it back to the media — The World-Herald's Dirk Chatelain.

Pelini called Eichorst vile names, some related to female genitalia, and bashed the overall culture of the athletic department. He said he'd rather work at McDonald's, that Husker fans are harder on players than LSU and Oklahoma fans are, that Eichorst was nothing more than a lawyer who made policies "to cover his own ass." It was a significant poisoning of the well right in the midst of Eichorst's search for a new coach.

Frost, fresh off Mariota's Heisman season, didn't get a phone call. He'd met Eichorst one summer before, taken a brief tour of the facilities, and had a conversation. But he wouldn't get one in 2014. What might have happened if Frost had taken over a team that Pelini groomed to distrust him?

Said Osborne in a recent interview: "I know he was disappointed he wasn't even contacted."

"I think he should be thankful we passed over him," Perlman says now, citing what Frost did at Central Florida. "And I think the fans should be."

As Pelini wrapped up his meeting with players, Eichorst, conducting his own one-man search, had already figured out his top choice to replace him. Mike Riley, the longtime Oregon State coach who'd never won a conference title — much less a national crown — was best known for staging occasional upsets of nationally ranked teams. Though Riley had turned laughing stock Oregon State into a respectable program, he wasn't a household name. And he wasn't on anyone's radar. Including Perlman's.

"I had to Google him," Perlman says. "I didn't know him before that."

Given his three failed seasons at Nebraska, Riley would be easy to forget — except for the fact that his failure, which brought the Huskers to their lowest point in a half-century — opened the door wide for Frost to come home.

Dec. 5, 2014: Nebraska introduces Mike Riley as the new head coach.

NEBRASKA FOOTBALL CAN'T GO ON LIKE THIS ANYMORE

BY DIRK CHATELAIN

LINCOLN — Somebody make it stop.

For the sake of all those national champions and All-Americans, for the millions who planned 55 years of fall weekends around a football schedule, for the thousands who grew up and grew old on the planks of Memorial Stadium, for the pride and dignity of a state and its flagship university.

Make. It. Stop.

Nebraska football can't go on like this anymore. Something's gotta give. Either the program gets better or its fans find something else to love. It's insane for 90,000 people to show up and get slapped in the face for 3½ hours.

Vegas oddsmakers projected a 24-point win for the road team Saturday, the biggest spread at Memorial Stadium in 60 years. Ohio State covered it in 27 minutes. By halftime, Urban Meyer had coached six quarters against Mike Riley dating back to last November. He'd scored 97 points to Riley's three.

At 35-0, Husker fans spilled out to Stadium Drive by the thousands. The flood included Travis Weiss, who used his dad's season tickets to take Amber Cameron on a first date.

"I felt like I took her to the worst movie ever," Weiss said.

They were still holding hands as they made their way toward downtown. What was the plan for the second half?

"Can't make out, because it wasn't a good movie," Weiss said.

Riley spoiled far more than a love story Saturday night. He surely lost his job, if not Sunday or Monday, then certainly in November. Nebraska fans will tolerate struggles. They won't tolerate indifference and incompetence. Those are defining characteristics of the 2017 Huskers and their coaching staff.

Saturday night was like descending a flight of stairs in the dark. You swear you've reached the bottom when — uh oh — there's four more steps. Crash.

Where's the floor for Nebraska?

"I'm a booster. I'm a season-ticket holder. But doggone it, this hurts," said an Omaha fan named Scott, who hasn't missed a home game since 1993. "You can't come into our stadium and run us out of there. C'mon."

Until a fourth-quarter turnover on downs, Ohio State had scored against the Blackshirts on 16 consecutive possessions — 14 touchdowns and two field goals — dating back to last year's game. The night was full of stunning stats like that, leaving impossible questions for Husker stakeholders.

You'd be crazy to think that 2½ years is enough time to build a program. Nebraska can't hit the reset button every few years. At some point, fans have to embrace a complete rebuilding process with all of its headaches and humiliations.

Maybe 10 years ago, the Huskers could hire a new coach and expect to vault back into the top 15. But the program is more Minnesota than Michigan now. Instability produces more instability. Patience is the only path forward.

And yet ...

You'd be crazy to think that Nebraska is close to a turnaround. All week, I've heard about Nebraska's recruiting improvements under Riley. How he's restocking the cupboard following Bo Pelini's recruiting neglect.

I don't need reminding that Riley inherited a weak roster. But watch the games, folks. The blue-chippers Nebraska does have — Lamar Jackson, Nick Gates, Jalin Barnett, Marquel Dismuke, Avery Anderson, etc. — aren't playing like it. And if Riley's underclassmen are so promising, why aren't more of them showing flashes now?

You're delusional if you think the Huskers are suddenly going to bust out in 2018. So how long do you give Riley to figure this out? Five years? You sure about that?

Go down the list of college football powerhouses. When they hire the right guy, change happens quickly. If not the first two seasons, then definitely in Year 3.

Bob Stoops. Jim Tressel. Urban Meyer. Pete Carroll. Chip Kelly. James Franklin. Chris Petersen. Mark Richt. They jolted the culture. They got results. Nebraska shouldn't be different.

For 40 years — 1962-2001 — NU didn't just lead the country in wins, it had 44 more wins than its closest pursuer, Penn State. Don't tell me they're no longer capable of competing with Wisconsin and Ohio State.

Start accepting weekly embarrassments and it's a sure path to long-term mediocrity.

But there are no easy answers here. Out on Stadium Drive, I came upon five guys discussing the future:

"There's no way he's back," Kyle Kruse said. "I think that's the final straw. Our worry is we have a chance at these four-star and five-star recruits."

"So Northern Illinois comes in, we had the 29th-ranked recruiting class, they had the 110th-ranked recruiting class," Taber Randolph said. "Who cares about a recruiting class if our coach can't coach worth a (expletive)."

"You lose if you do, you lose if you don't," Joe Wallace said. "Next year is going to be messed up anyway. They might be 5-7. Maybe."

"That schedule is stupid hard," Kruse said.

"You gotta get the big-name coach, man," Scott Wise said. "Look at what (Jim) Harbaugh did in one year. It's all about the coaching, I'm telling you."

"It really is tough when you see (Scott) Frost. He took 0-12, then 6-6, and now just tonight, he's kicking the (expletive) out of East Carolina," Kruse said.

"But he's in Florida," Wise said. "That's where all the talent's at."

"UCF, 42-14 at halftime," Matt Nelson said.

"That's Scotty doing work," Kruse said.

Those discussions will fill the coffee shops and text chains for the next two weeks. But the real work belongs to Hank Bounds, Ronnie Green and the new Nebraska athletic director.

They don't need to take Husker football back to 1995. They do need to restore pride and dignity to Memorial Stadium. They need to prevent nights like Saturday from ever happening again.

As the clock expired on the worst home loss since 1949, as Mike Riley walked off the field for perhaps the last time on a game day, Nebraska's remaining fans were rewarded for their patience.

A clear path to the exits.

Oct. 14, 2017: Coach Mike Riley leaves the field after losing 56-14 to Ohio State at Memorial Stadium.

RILEY STILL LIES IN BED sometimes and thinks about what he could have done better at Nebraska. His three years — 6-7, 9-4, 4-8 — were the worst three-year stretch of Husker football since the Bill Jennings era.

But even he has to concede ...

"It's the right fit with Scott," Riley said in an interview for this book. Even if it took Riley through some of the lowest lows of his career, Nebraska appears on its best track in many, many years.

It's a track that, at the start of NU's 2017 football season, didn't seem likely.

After years at Oregon, Frost had taken the Central Florida headcoaching job and taken over a team that was winless the season before. The Knights had quit, in effect, on their former coach, George O'Leary, who had led Central Florida to a Fiesta Bowl win just two seasons before. Frost knew there was talent — and ease of recruiting — in Orlando, and jumped at that job instead of Power Five coaching offers he had on the table. Frost finished 6-7 in 2016 — a vast improvement from 0-12. Still, Central Florida wasn't favored to win the American Athletic Conference title in 2017, and Nebraska seemed likely

Sept. 3, 2016: Scott leads his Central Florida team onto the field before playing South Carolina State in Orlando.

to churn out seven or eight wins in Riley's third season. That'd be enough to keep a much-praised recruiting class together and give Riley a deciding fourth year.

Nebraska's season collapsed swiftly. As Frost's team had a game canceled by Hurricane Irma, Riley stepped in the eye of his own storm when NU lost at Oregon and, one week later, to Northern Illinois. Eichorst — who'd stubbed his toe too many times with media, other Husker coaches and people in his own administration — was fired by his university bosses, President Hank Bounds and Chancellor Ronnie Green.

"I knew all that was not good," Riley said with a chuckle.

It got worse. Wisconsin whipped Nebraska 38-17. Ohio State scored on eight straight drives in a 56-14 blowout that looked so effortless that it made the Huskers look like a high school program. Fans fled the scene, just as they had for the 2007 Oklahoma State game. As interim A.D. and Husker legend Dave Rimington questioned Riley on the strength of the walk-on program — and Riley's newly-hired defensive coordinator, Bob Diaco, bent reporters' ears with curious quotes — Bounds and Green hired a football A.D., Washington State's Bill Moos, to grade Riley and, surely everyone knew, hire a new coach.

Bounds and Green pointed Moos to Osborne, always watchful, always willing to lend a word. And Osborne pointed Moos to the radio color commentator for Nebraska's football games, Matt Davison, who had caught Frost's most-famous pass, "the flea kicker" in the 1997 game against Missouri. Davison had witnessed the full ugliness of the Riley era and the bumps and bruises of the Bo era.

He was also one of Frost's best friends. If Riley's inner circle was sprawling enough to encompass a suburb — that was part of his weakness — Frost kept a tighter counsel. Davison was close — a golfing buddy, a confidant — who'd even watched in person Central Florida's first game of 2017. Frost said Davison was "pestering" him to return. Frost, not swayed by easy sentiment, consumed by Central Florida's undefeated run, is the kind of man who needs a little pestering to listen.

Nov. 24, 2017: Mike Riley leaves the field following the Huskers' 56-14 loss to Iowa at Memorial Stadium. Riley is fired the next day but stays upbeat. "I loved the opportunity to coach here," he said.

By the time Nebraska lost to Northwestern in overtime — and the fastidious Diaco, leaning against a counter, was telling reporters there was "no reasonable reason" the Huskers' hideous defense should be expected to do any better than it was — Nebraska's team was ready for a coaching change. Especially that hapless defense, confused and frustrated by Diaco's military-style methods and exacting speechifying. The Blackshirts — hardly that — gave up 54, 56 and 56 points in their last three games.

After the 54-21 loss at Minnesota, Moos told Davison to set up a meeting in Philadelphia, where Central Florida was playing Temple. Moos could fly in, meet with Frost in a hotel, and fly to Nebraska's game at Penn State. Moos brought along his wife, Kendra, who could play hostess. As The World-Herald's

Henry Cordes' six-part saga on The Return of Scott Frost recounted, the meeting was the moment Moos sold Frost on their future together.

Most poignantly, Frost during the meeting spoke directly about how much it hurt for him to see that Nebraska football was no longer the program he'd grown up loving and playing for.

He noted critical elements to the program's past success that had become lost or diminished, including the program's "championship mentality" and passion to be the best. Frost questioned whether that could be restored.

Moos assured Frost he wanted to bring back that mindset. "I have a championship mentality," he said. "I didn't come to Nebraska to be 4-6 in November."

NUMBERS FROM THE DECLINE

The contrast is stark when the numbers from the Tom Osborne era are compared to the numbers from the last 20 years of Husker football.

- Nebraska lost three home games in the 1990s — two of them to eventual national champions. Since joining the Big Ten in 2011, the Huskers have lost 12 home games, including a whopping five in 2017.

- For the entire 1980s, Nebraska never lost a game by more than 24 points — a 41-17 loss to Florida State in the Fiesta Bowl that technically took place on Jan. 1, 1990. In the last two seasons alone, Nebraska has had five losses more than 25 points — 62-3 to Ohio State in 2016, 40-10 to Iowa in 2016, 56-14 to Ohio State in 2017, 54-21 to Minnesota in 2017 and 56-14 to Iowa in 2017.

- During its 1997 national title run, Nebraska's defense gave up 73.4 rushing yards per game and 2.2 yards per carry. In 2017, opponents nearly tripled both of those numbers, averaging 216.7 rushing yards per game and 5.7 yards per carry.

- Nebraska averaged 392.6 rushing yards per game in 1997. In 2017? An anemic result — 107.5 yards per game, which ranked 120th in the nation.

- In 2013 and 2014, Ameer Abdullah ran for more yards by himself than Nebraska did as a team in 2017.

- From 1982 through the 1997 season — the full flowering of Tom Osborne's option offense — Nebraska ranked among college football's top ten scoring offenses every year, finishing No. 1 in 1982, 1983, 1995 and 1997. The season that broke the streak: 1998. Frank Solich's first year. While Nebraska returned to the top ten in 2000 and 2001, the Huskers haven't since.

- In Osborne's last three seasons as head coach, his teams gave up a combined total of 14 sacks. Over three seasons! NU gave up 20 alone in 1998, Frank Solich's first year.

- Melvin Gordon averaged 16.32 yards per carry in Wisconsin's 59-24 romp over the Huskers in 2014. He didn't play the fourth quarter and still rushed for 408 yards. But that yards-per-average wasn't Gordon's best against Nebraska. Nope — he gained 24 yards per tote in the 2012 Big Ten Championship, rushing for 216 yards — on all of nine carries.

- Scott Frost had more than 1,000 yards rushing and 1,000 yards passing in 1997. In his 2001 Heisman season, Eric Crouch did the same, as did Jammal Lord in 2002. Since then, only one Husker quarterback — Taylor Martinez — has done it.

- The Blackshirts had 44 sacks in the 1997 national title season. In 2017, that number dwindled down to 14. No Power Five conference team had fewer, and only one other P5 had 14. Oregon State.

- Nebraska hasn't finished ranked in the final Associated Press top 10 since the 2001 season. Since then, NU's highest postseason AP ranking is 14th in 2009. The other years NU was ranked: 19th in 2003, 24th in 2005, 20th in 2010, 24th in 2011 and 25th in 2012. Iowa, by contrast, has been ranked in the postseason AP poll six times since 2001 — and in the top ten four times since 2001.

- After Nebraska had a +23 turnover margin in 2003 — Bo Pelini's lone year as Nebraska's defensive coordinator — the Huskers were a cumulative -31 in turnover margin during the Bill Callahan era, -33 during the seven years Pelini was head coach, and -14 during the Mike Riley era. From 2004-2017, Nebraska had just two seasons with a positive turnover margin — 2009(+5) and 2016(+5).

- In the last decade, Nebraska's highest-rated recruiting class was the 2011 bunch, which was considered a top-20 class nationally. Out of that class, 11 of the signees either didn't make it to campus or finished their college careers at a different school. Though the class produced the best overall Husker of the Big Ten era — Ameer Abdullah — it otherwise fell apart.

- Husker football used to be elite at scoring defensive and special teams touchdowns. The 1999 team, for example, scored six non-offensive touchdowns. Mike Riley's three teams scored a six touchdowns combined. In three years under Riley, Nebraska did not return a punt for a touchdown.

- At the time Colorado scored 62 points on Nebraska in 2001, it was a watershed moment, the most points ever scored against a Husker team. Since then, Nebraska has allowed 70 points twice, 65 points, 63 points and 62 points twice more and a whopping 76 points to Kansas in 2007, which left then-defensive coordinator Kevin Cosgrove teary-eyed after the game.

- Since joining the Big Ten, Nebraska is 6-16 against Associated Press poll ranked opponents. Over Tom Osborne's last five seasons in the 1990s, NU finished 18-2.

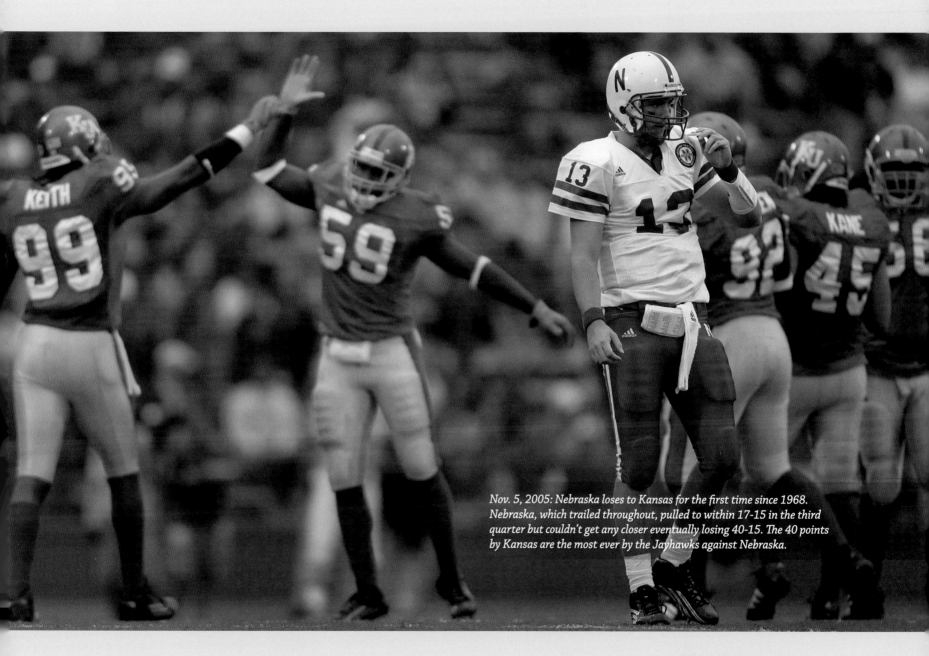

Nov. 5, 2005: Nebraska loses to Kansas for the first time since 1968. Nebraska, which trailed throughout, pulled to within 17-15 in the third quarter but couldn't get any closer eventually losing 40-15. The 40 points by Kansas are the most ever by the Jayhawks against Nebraska.

HE GREW UP ON THE campus. His mom and dad competed there. He originally spurned Nebraska, then relented, returning to Lincoln to play two fateful seasons in Lincoln. In so many ways, Frost was tied to this place, and the time was right for his return. He was a coach on the rise who had turned 0-12 into a 12-0 regular season. He'd be the guy Tennessee and Florida wanted, but couldn't get. He'd be the architect of a cutting-edge offense.

> **"IF I GO THERE AND FAIL, I WON'T HAVE ANY HOME. I WON'T BE ABLE TO STAY, AND I WILL HAVE GIVEN UP MY HOME HERE."**
>
> — SCOTT FROST TO ORLANDO TV SPORTS ANCHOR PAT CLARKE

Perhaps if Nebraska were coming off a 20-year run with Frank Solich as coach, Frost's hiring would have been a cinch.

But Frost had to say yes to Nebraska knowing all the damage that had been done to the Husker brand. Knowing all the petty fights and blowout losses and strange politics of the place. Riley said he felt it the whole time he was coaching the Huskers. People making impulsive decisions out of fear, then overcorrecting. Fans taking sides. Pelini was perhaps wrong that Nebraska is harder than all other college football jobs, but it is hard. The fishbowl is real. And Frost didn't have one at Central Florida. As he explained to an Orlando TV reporter before he took the Nebraska job, he could be anonymous there.

Not here. Not at Nebraska. The stakes are in the ground, the legacy has already been discussed. A state leans in hoping this is the time when it all aligns.

Frost had doubts. Of the many people he could share them with he chose Pat Clarke, an Orlando TV sports anchor. He laid out the dilemma and said he had two homes — one in Orlando and one with Larry and Carol in Nebraska.

"If I go there and fail, I won't have any home," Frost told Clarke. "I won't be able to stay, and I will have given up my home here."

Failure is not an option for Frost. Not like it was for Riley, who never gave up his home near Oregon State's campus. He took an assistant coaching job at OSU after his firing at NU and even rode his bike — through the rain — to the first practice, like he always used to do. Riley left home and went home again, although by June 2018 he was gone again to coach San Antonio in a new spring professional league, the Alliance of American Football.

Nebraska's not a job you leave. You either stay, and become legend, or you fail, and the search for the next Osborne continues.

So while Frost — on the Monday before he took the job, the Monday after Moos fired Riley — agreed to the Husker job, he had doubts, too. Those lingered until a final call with his coach, Osborne, the Friday night before Central Florida played for the American Athletic Conference title against Memphis.

Dec. 2, 2017: Scott perhaps was pondering his future during a press conference following the American Athletic Conference championship game when his Central Florida Knights beat Memphis in an overtime thriller, 62-55.

Frost relayed his concerns. Osborne countered with an undeniable truth: If he wanted to win a national title — and he did — he could do it at Nebraska. Central Florida stood little chance with a College Football Playoff that sandbagged the Knights' ranking in the CFP poll so much that Frost had no chance of making the playoff in Orlando.

"This thing came up quicker than either of us thought, but here it is," Osborne told him that night. "Maybe 10 years from now, whoever they hire is still going to be here. If this is something you want to do, now is probably the time."

Two days later, Frost was back in Nebraska, trying to sort through his emotions. While a state celebrated, Frost just tried to navigate the moment. He was married now to Ashley Neidhardt. They had welcomed their first child, a son, on Nov. 8. The team he was coaching had just won a conference crown. His dream job — the one he was made to have — was his.

From left, University of Nebraska-Lincoln Chancellor Ronnie Green, NU Athletic Director Bill Moos, University of Nebraska President Hank Bounds and Tom Osborne pose for photographers with Scott, center, after he was introduced as Nebraska's new coach.

Jan. 1, 2018: Scott hoists the Peach Bowl trophy after his Central Florida Knights beat Auburn 34-27 to cap an undefeated (13-0) season.

Jan. 1, 2018: Scott celebrates with his players after winning the Peach Bowl.

For a month, he balanced recruiting for Nebraska with coaching Central Florida to its Peach Bowl win. His strength coach, Zach Duval, has a blend of new-age teachings and old-school Husker Power roots. Frost also brought his entire coaching and support staff with him from Central Florida.

"If they're good enough to take a 0-12 program to 13-0 in two years, they're good enough to coach anywhere — because what they accomplished at Central Florida is next to impossible," Frost said in December.

The staff has gone on multiple fan tours of the state, sitting in country clubs, bars and convention halls. Frost — more circumspect — has made the occasional appearances. They've survived spring practice and the media onslaught that comes with being Nebraska's head coach. Frost enjoyed a sold-out spring game, and the version of The Beatles' "Come Together" blared over the speakers during the Tunnel Walk. Frost's spread, no-huddle, fast-paced offense is expected to make waves. The Husker defense is expected to be aggressive. Frost preaches constantly to his players: Don't fear failure. Take your shot. Trust your instincts.

The same could be said for Frost's leap of faith into the Nebraska head coaching job. He's a former player and a native son — a combination, in this way, of Osborne and Solich. Fans have been waiting years for his return. And now it's here.

This spring, Frost was asked what fans say to him on the street. Do they put their expectations on him? Do they convey their hope for a full resurrection of Husker football?

Frost said they do not. Of course they don't. They're Nebraskans. They tell him "Welcome home," or "We're glad you're back."

That's an easy one for Frost to answer.

"That's great to hear, because I'm glad I'm back, too," Frost said. "This is home. The state of Nebraska — and the people I know and care about — is going to make the job even more rewarding."

Sports apparel features welcome-home messages for Scott, in anticipation of Frost's first season as head coach.

June 11, 2018: Kim Hinrichsen of Cheyenne, Wyoming, takes a selfie with Scott at the Gering Civic Center in Gering, Nebraska, during a coaches' tour of the state.

SPOILER ALERT: THIS IS GOING TO BE FUN

BY TOM SHATEL

FEB. 4, 2020, ST. PAUL, NEBRASKA

The cars started lining up on Howard Avenue at about 9 a.m., and by 10 there were minor traffic back-ups on Highway 281 coming into town. They came from the farms and the small towns, in new red pick-ups and old white ones. They were farmers, middle-aged insurance men, mechanics and moms holding kids. Those who couldn't park across the street from the school settled for a few blocks away and walked up to the corner, where they could get a glimpse of Scott Frost arriving at the high school to recruit the big boy left tackle who had dreamed of this moment his whole life. Heck, in this central Nebraska hamlet, they all had.

OCT. 2, 2021, LINCOLN

On an Indian summer Saturday, Scott Frost landed his first big one.

It went by the name of Urban Meyer. And after a breathless day in which classic, high-stakes football returned to Memorial Stadium, nobody would blame Frost if he had the game mounted and framed in his office.

For three hours, the Huskers and Ohio State Buckeyes went back and forth, punching and counter-punching though at times it seemed that Meyer and Frost were in the ring alone, throwing haymakers from play books.

The Big Ten king and the man who would be king.

All hail the new king. Frost's Huskers out-punched and out-lasted the mighty Bucks, 24-21, in a game that old-timers were calling the hardest-hitting football game they'd seen on this field since the Oklahoma game in 1978.

Tom Osborne earned his Nebraska coaching stripes that day, and here, a generation and conference away, it seemed that Frost had done the same.

It took some magic, on a 75-yard drive that ate up nearly all of the final three minutes, with senior quarterback Adrian Martinez pulling third-down rabbit after rabbit out of his hat. The drama wound down to a crucial third-and-4 at the Ohio State 7, in which Martinez faked a keeper and pitched to a slot receiver coming the other way on a reverse.

"We had the play scouted, but they fooled us," Meyer said. "Hats off to them."

Nebraska moved into the driver's seat in the Big Ten West, with home games upcoming against Michigan, Iowa and Wisconsin.

"This was a great win," Frost told the media. "But nobody should be celebrating anything. We have a tough game with Northwestern next week. We haven't done anything yet."

DEC. 2, 2028, INDIANAPOLIS

They won. Now they wait.

Scott Frost won his third Big Ten champion-ship on Saturday night at Lucas Oil Stadium, pounding Michigan, 35-14. But as the Huskers gathered on the award stand to collect their tro-phy, most fans, players and coaches had already turned their attention to the long 12 hours that awaited the team.

Nebraska, 13-0, sat fifth in the College Football Playoff standings — behind No. 1 Alabama, No. 2 Texas, No. 3 USC and No. 4 Florida. The Huskers figured to move ahead of one-loss Florida, but the Gators knocked off previous-ly-unbeaten Alabama in the SEC championship game — providing a dilemma for the Playoff Committee and chairman Steve Spurrier.

Asked about the situation by a Fox Sports reporter during the award ceremony, Frost shrugged and said, "I don't have too much to say. I think we just made a pretty good case on the field. I'm proud of my team and we'll play anybody."

But the MVP of the Big Ten title game, quar-terback Jimmy Chitwood, grabbed the mic and said, "If you can vote for Florida or Alabama in good conscience after what you saw, go ahead. But if you watched our game tonight, I don't know how anyone can deny this great man a chance at a national championship."

June 15, 2018: Scott watches drills during the Friday Night Lights camp at Memorial Stadium.

OH YEAH, THIS IS going to be fun.

We hope you've enjoyed this book. It's been a labor of love to share our experiences, stories, columns and photos.

This book isn't hype. It's history.

It's the story of Scott Frost's early life as a Nebraska kid and quarterback, born and raised by a mother and father who both were athletes and coaches. From Wood River to national champion.

And now head football coach at the University of Nebraska.

It's an incredible story. It's the story of Nebraska. The Nebraska Dream, in many ways.

And we're just getting started.

What are we about to watch here? The expectations, hyperbole and excitement are off the charts for the Frost Era. A return to conference and national championships. Relevance.

But it makes sense, because of Frost's journey. His upbringing. His education. His training at the hands of Osborne, Walsh, Parcells and Kelly — not to mention Larry and Carol.

It's as if Frost was born to be the Nebraska football coach. And at the risk of falling off the cliff, I'll go it one further.

He's got the makings of a Nebraska coaching icon.

That's a risky statement, because there aren't many icons in college football anymore. Legends. Coaches who were known by one name.

Bear. Bob. Tom. Joe. Bobby. Barry.

Today, it's Saban. Urban. One of these days there might be a Dabo.

You don't see as many anymore, for a couple of reasons. One, Nick Saban isn't good at sharing the national championship. Two, a lot of coaches don't stay long enough to become legends. They win and chase the money and the next job. And, boosters are less patient than ever. It's hard to grow icons these days.

But if there is a guy positioned to one day be more powerful than the governor of Nebraska, or shut down St. Paul on a slow Tuesday in February, it's Frost.

Frost is uniquely qualified to be an icon, even more than Saban or Urban or Osborne or Devaney.

As powerful as he is, Saban isn't from Alabama and didn't play there. Meyer didn't play at Ohio State. Osborne is Hastings-born but also never wore the Husker uniform.

Frost grew up here and played here. He takes over a demanding job that isn't for the meek. He takes over a program that works best with certain philosophies in place. He coaches for a fan base that is fiercely loyal so long as you give them what they want.

Frost knows the passwords better than anyone. He's lived here, played here, done that.

And that will give him a dashing head start in accomplishing the first priority of his coaching tenure: Bring Nebraska football back to the state of Nebraska again. Restore the pride. Make folks feel good about being a Husker fan.

Sure, Nebraskans want to be stars on the national stage again. Recruiting on both coasts and every stop in between matters a bunch.

But it's a fact that when Big Red was winning and dominating all those Devaney-Osborne years, the program was a force because the state was unified. All on board the train barreling down the tracks.

From Auburn to Alliance to the farms to the cities to the top of South Stadium and to the school president's suite and down to the sideline. All pushing in one direction.

Toward January. Toward glory.

It's set up to return to that and Frost is the one who holds the key. Look around Nebraska in the early months of the Frost Era. The state is ready to explode.

But you know how we'll know? The kids at Nebraska's middle schools will show us the way.

In the last several years, I've had two daughters attend middle school. And every day at drop-off, I felt like I was watching the College Football Playoff.

I saw shirts and sweatshirts and hats. Oregon. Oklahoma. Alabama. Texas. Ohio State. Kansas (basketball, of course).

Very, very rarely did you ever see a kid wearing a Husker shirt.

If the young folks in this state don't know you, or don't want to acknowledge you, you've got problems.

There was a day when any kid wearing an Oklahoma or Texas shirt would be scolded by his buddies into going home and changing.

That's already changing, and it's because of one coach, the hottest young coach in the country, who dons Yeezys and promises a return to making Nebraska great again.

Kids will show us the way. And they are already lining up behind Frost.

"I just had a conversation with my 15-year-old and his buddies," said Matt Hoskinson, the Nebraska offensive lineman from 1994-97 who lives in Omaha.

"His question to me was: 'Why are we getting these recruits and why are we getting this attention? What is Scott doing differently?'

"I don't think the answer is that complicated. We have a young, hot coach. The best available. Any school that had an opening wanted him. It just so happens he played football at Nebraska and is a home-town kid. All these things are coming together at the right time.

"Nebraska kids, including my own children, have never seen Nebraska be good in football. If they're going to get that opportunity, I think we're going to see a change. I think we're seeing that already."

Build up from the inside-out. Stoke the fires within the borders. Make Husker football relevant in Nebraska. Create demand and buzz. Put that passion in a blender and turn it on high.

"I think you're going to see a return to not just excitement everywhere, but belief," Hoskinson said. "Scott has to execute on the back end of that. You're going to get some good players. You have to win some games. I think Scott will get that done."

Keep the best players in the state home. The kids on the outside looking in will pay attention. What's the buzz all about? Got to find out.

There's a generation out there that doesn't know Nebraska won national championships. But that generation also doesn't know what it's like to see the state on fire for college football. Really on fire.

Winning does that. Winning big. But so does playing football the Nebraska Way. Developing starters. Walk-ons who make plays. Going hard for four quarters. Being tough and physical. A blue collar beneath a red jersey.

Going back to the Husker "Business Plan" figures to work. And doing things the Nebraska way will buy Frost time and patience from folks who crave a team they're proud to root for — win, lose or win.

Frost knows he'll have to win, that it's the only way this will work out, but he embraced that a long time ago. And that's what gives him his best chance.

The world has changed. Everyone in college football is on television. Everyone has a giant weight room. Everyone has stuff. But college football isn't about stuff.

It's about the head coach.

Having a difference-maker head coach, and the mystique that goes with it, separates the contenders from the pretenders in college football. You've either got it or you don't.

When you're in the middle of America and you have to get on planes to recruit, you need all the head coaching mystique you can get.

It helps to have a guy who fits into that mold as comfortably as an old shoe. Or a new Yeezy.

Frost has not only been around coaching and coaches his whole life, he's lived with the expectations. He comes at this task with a cocksure attitude and confidence that might rub strangers the wrong way. But those who know Frost understand.

Frost thinks he's going to win and he doesn't mind telling you and, frankly, doesn't care what you think.

That sort of thing comes in awfully handy at a job like Nebraska. While many coaches have gotten claustrophobic in the fish bowl, Frost will treat it like a 10-room mansion with a pool and basketball court.

In other words, the bigger the job, the higher the bar, the more comfortable Frost will feel in this environment. Also known as "home."

A new generation of Nebraska may get to see what it was like under Devaney and Osborne. Where the entire state gathered around to watch every game, every move. Goodness, some may even put their phones down.

I'm a hopeless college football romantic. I loved the days of college football icons. I embrace the idea of the coach driving into small towns and watching the folks leave their offices and homes to go catch a glimpse of the head football coach setting foot in their town.

In the next several years, I think there will be diners, Elks Lodges, country clubs and schools with photos of Frost on the wall, posing with local officials or teachers or just good, plain folks.

And those will go next to their father's photos of Devaney at the Moose Lodge or Osborne with his plate of meatloaf talking to the ranchers.

There's an old-school charm there, but in Nebraska, I think it's completely necessary to the overall goal. It's the base, the foundation. And I think it makes Nebraska football better.

"I'll never forget the day Coach Osborne came to Battle Creek to visit me at the school," Hoskinson said. "The whole town knew about it. There was a buzz.

"When he came to the school, it was a scene. It was an event. It's Battle Creek. There's 1,000 people in it. It was a big deal. There were local farmers, everybody around there, hanging around. I'm kind of proud of it, too. That's the way small towns are in this state.

"Scott is going to have that very early. I think he'll be able to do it much earlier than anyone else could. And I think he'll have a bigger impact (in the state) than Mike Riley, Bill Callahan, Bo Pelini, even Frank Solich.

"It's a presence. Scott draws people to him. He's already won but he's only been a head coach for two years. But he has a reputation and the fact that he's going to walk into schools, the school is going to stop. They're going to feel that.

"He's going to have the same impact as Coach Osborne."

That's the expectation in a lot of corners, and it's unbelievable and yet natural. And it makes what we're about to see all the more compelling. And exciting.

Devaney didn't have that when he arrived in 1962. He had won at Wyoming, but wasn't from here. Mostly, there wasn't the expectation for the program then. Devaney had to build it from the ground up.

Osborne inherited incredibly high standards when he replaced Devaney in 1973. The Huskers had won national titles in 1970 and 1971 and expectations were that the program wouldn't drop as a national power.

And though Osborne was known as a long-time assistant under Devaney, that wasn't necessarily positive. There was a lot of uncertainty about how a first-time head coach would do behind the wheel of this machine. Some fans wanted Monte Kiffin to get the job. There wasn't universal agreement.

Frost inherits a program that went 4-8, yet he's being greeted by championship expectations. Not this year. But certainly down the road. And Frost welcomes those expectations, agrees with them.

Throw in his new-school education under Chip Kelly at Oregon, to go with his old-school football diploma from Osborne, and it adds to the intrigue. We don't know what we're about to witness. But we think, hope, yes, expect it to be special.

I'm not sure there has been anything like this in Nebraska football history.

If you're into history, take notes. Savor everything. It feels like something important is about to happen.

Can Frost combine the philosophies of Osborne and Kelly and bring Nebraska back to the cutting edge? Will he be a charming icon like Devaney? Will he be more like the brilliant chess master Osborne?

Or will the first Scott Frost carve his own legend and forge his own path, and where will that take us?

This is the end of the book. But the story is just beginning.

April 21, 2018: Husker fan Kian Morris, 9, of Wilber, Nebraska, passes a football before the Husker spring game.

PHOTO INDEX

A T-shirt welcoming Scott home.